REFORMING
THE REFORMS

REFORMING THE REFORMS

A Critical Analysis of the Presidential Selection Process

JAMES W. CEASER

BALLINGER PUBLISHING COMPANY
Cambridge, Massachusetts
A Subsidiary of Harper & Row, Publishers, Inc.

International Standard Book Number: 0–88410–884–8

Library of Congress Catalog Card Number: 81–21638

Printed in the United States of America

Library of Congress Cataloging in Publication Data

Ceaser, James W.
  Reforming the reforms.

  Includes bibliographical references and index.
  1. Presidents—United States—Nomination. I. Title.
JK521.C4   324.5'0973   81–21638
ISBN 0–88410–884–8   AACR2

To Jennifer

Many daughters have done virtuously, but thou excellest them all.

Proverbs

CONTENTS

LIST OF FIGURES AND TABLES

ACKNOWLEDGMENTS

I would like to thank the Twentieth Century Fund for its support in writing this book and for the assistance of the editor, Beverly Goldberg. William Connelly helped greatly with the research and provided numerous comments and suggestions that I incorporated into the book. I also profited from the many helpful criticisms of the graduate students in my seminars at the University of Virginia. Finally, my thanks to my wife, Blaire, for her patience, support, and encouragement during the last year.

1 INTRODUCTION

American politics has just passed through an extraordinary era of reform, the consequences of which have been as profound as those of the reform period that accompanied the Progressive movement earlier in this century. No major national institution, with the possible exception of the Supreme Court, has escaped the influence of the recent reforms, and their effects are certain to continue—and perhaps to increase—throughout this decade, even as the impetus for reform begins to diminish.

The movement for reform first came to national prominence at the strife-torn 1968 Democratic convention in Chicago. Antiwar activists and advocates of the "New Politics" launched an attack not only on the nation's party system and method of nominating presidential candidates but also, in some measure, on the entire structure of American representative institutions. The spirit of reform, moderated in the hands of political leaders in the Democratic party and Congress, quickly gathered momentum, dominating much of the rhetoric of the last decade and all but compelling many in public life to offer unqualified praise of democracy and openness. In the name of reform, the nominating system was changed from a predominantly representative process, in which delegates and party leaders had the final say in choosing the nominees, to a process based on the principle of direct democracy, in which the voters in primaries determined the results. The reform movement spread to Congress, where

1

power in the House was dispersed and diffused and where committee deliberations in both the House and Senate were opened up to
unprecedented publicity. In the electoral process, reformers helped
pass legislation governing campaign financing for federal offices that
limited campaign contributions and provided public funding for presidential campaigns. Finally, certain reformers attempted—unsuccess-
fully—to enact constitutional amendments for direct election of the
president and for establishing a mechanism for national referendums.

By the end of the 1970s, however, the American political clime
began to change. Whatever the benefits of the reforms, experience
with their consequences led many to conclude that they also made
the task of governing more difficult and fell far short of realizing
most of their original objectives. By the 1980 Democratic convention, many former advocates of reform had become disillusioned,
finding that the "open" system of presidential nominations that they
had instituted produced a "closed" or nondeliberative result. Sentiment among political leaders quickly turned against further reforms,
and shortly reform rhetoric all but disappeared from American politics. By the end of 1980, House Majority Leader Thomas P. (Tip)
O'Neill, Jr., spoke of the "reform pendulum swinging back," and the
then chairman of the Democratic National Party, John White, asked
the party's National Committee to consider numerous "corrections"
of the earlier party reforms. The governing precepts of the reform
movement, if not discredited, were no longer considered unassaila-
ble doctrine, and a period of intense questioning and reexamination
began. For all intents and purposes, the reform era has now ended.

Movements as broad as reform defy simple characterization. During periods when they dominate public discussion, various political
forces attempt to identify with them and march under their banner,
and only in retrospect is it possible to sort out all the tendencies that
contributed to their development. In spite of this complexity, these
movements usually begin with a single impulse that provides the
theme around which people organize and justify their activities to
the general public. Seen in this light, the reform movement of the
last decade got under way as an effort to establish the principles of
democracy and openness as the standards by which to judge the legitimacy of American political institutions. The movement called into
question those aspects of our political institutions that involved quiet
group accommodations within traditional representative processes,
and it held that the public interest could be served only by institu-

tions that were democratic in their procedures and open to public observation.

Viewed in historical perspective, the reform effort of the last decade, like the Progressive movement, was another in a long series of conflicts between two interpretations of the fundamental American principle of the "consent of the governed": direct democracy (or populism) and representative decisionmaking. These two interpretations should be understood more as impulses than fully elaborated concepts, for neither one constitutes a totally distinct or coherent theory of governing. The impulse for representative decisionmaking is based on the idea of granting discretionary judgment to institutions whose representatives act on behalf of the public or an association of the public. In practice, of course, any method of selecting representatives usually produces certain informal commitments, even where laws do not bind the representative to any particular decision. The representative impulse, however, seeks not only to protect the representatives' legal right to discretion, but also to institute general arrangements that in fact enable representatives to exercise their judgment. Direct democracy, by contrast, is characterized by the tendency to allow the people to make decisions. In the perfect case, direct democracy is illustrated by decisionmaking in town meetings, or—to speculate on future possibilities—through two-way television on which citizens may express their preferences on public issues. By extension, direct democracy is found in mechanisms for making decisions by elections, as in referenda or in the binding of representatives to specific decisions. More generally, the democratic impulse is expressed in the tendency to reduce the discretion of a representative body and make its decisions subject to the immediate influence or determination of popular pressure.

The reforms of the last decade had their greatest impact, in terms of promoting the democratic impulse, in the nominating process. It was here, at the point of origin of the reform movement, that reformers managed to transform completely—and not just to modify—a major national political process. In itself, a change from representative to democratic decisionmaking cannot be considered either good or bad. The election of the American president, which under the Constitution was designed originally to be a representative process, was quickly changed, and no one today questions the result. Both the democratic and representative impulses have deep roots in the American political tradition, and the merits of each cannot be judged in the abstract but must be weighed in every case in light of their potential effects.

Judging from the recent criticism of the nominating system, the new and democratic method has failed to win the confidence of the American public and its leaders. According to a leading scholar of political parties, Austin Ranney, "There is today more dissatisfaction with the nature of the process by which we choose our presidential candidates than there has been at any time since the late 1960s."[1] Commentators from all points on the political spectrum, including many who were the staunchest supporters of reform over the last decade, have argued that the nominating system that has evolved since 1968 is so illogical in its structure and damaging in its effects that further change of a fundamental kind is needed. Legislators[2] and party leaders, accordingly, face a critical choice in the years ahead. Either they will devise a more satisfactory method of nomination that is based on (or extends) the prevailing principle of direct democracy, or they will institute—some would say reinstitute—a system that is based on representative decisionmaking.

Discussion of this choice began at the 1980 Democratic convention in the debate on the so-called open convention. Although charged with all the intensity of a political battle, the debate still served to bring before the American public the major theoretical issues in the dispute between direct democracy and representation. One group, which included President Carter's supporters, defended the principle of direct democracy to the point of denying the delegates any discretion whatsoever when voting for the presidential nominee. According to the advocates of this view, the people's decision was final and should not be subject to review by a representative assembly. A second group, which included Senator Edward Kennedy's supporters and many of the original proponents of reform, found itself in the sometimes embarrassing position of defending the traditional prerogative of representative bodies to act at their own discretion, irrespective of instructions purporting to bind delegates. This second group argued that a representative assembly, properly labeled, must have the right to exercise independent judgment.

While this debate forced many to reconsider their automatic commitment to direct democracy, in practical terms it dealt with only the relatively minor issue of a party rule that enforced commitments that delegates had already made. As most participants probably realized, the real issues about direct democracy and representation were much deeper and involved the more fundamental question of whether the process *as a whole* should be geared to a popular choice of the nominee or whether the delegates—including major party leaders and elected officials—should have the discretion to make their own selection. It is this broader question of the role of parties and representative decisionmaking in the nominating process that confronts legislators today.[3]

No one, of course, should be under the illusion that legislators can fully direct and regulate the course of institutional development. Institutions are not transformed by acts of legislation and rulemaking alone; they grow and change with the times as they interact constantly with their environment. Factors that lie outside of the immediate control of legislators, ranging from technological innovations in communications to broad shifts in political values, limit choice and shape the evolution of institutions in unforeseen ways. Yet deliberate attempts to legislate change, if undertaken at the right moment and with an awareness of the historical circumstances, often can succeed in determining the broad outlines of an institution's development in the next era.

These favorable conditions, it appears, exist today. Not only has a consensus emerged that change of some kind is needed, but legislators and scholars have been able to profit from the recent period of institutional instability by learning more about the nominating process and the difficulties involved in making changes to achieve planned objectives. Compared with the years when reform first began, today there is more room for serious deliberation and less a sense of acting under the threat of an imminent crisis. Experience has made people wary of the vague slogans that swayed participants in earlier debates, and legislators are looking at current proposals for change with much greater care.

To understand how we reached this critical point in the development of the nominating process, it is necessary to look briefly at the nominating system before the recent reform era. The "mixed" selection system that existed before 1968 combined in an uneasy but relatively stable balance the two principles of representative decisionmaking and direct democracy. The representative component of the system, which then was clearly the dominant of the two, allowed the delegates to act on their own or at the direction of local party leaders. The origins of the representative component can be traced back to the beginning of the convention system in the early nineteenth century, when the state parties had the authority to devise their rules of delegate selection and generally used it to establish systems that protected the delegates' discretion. Under the mixed system, which developed in the 1920s, representative decisionmaking found its institutional support in states that chose their delegates in party-run conventions; in primary states where delegate selection was separated from national candidate competition; and, of course, in the national convention itself, which offered a setting for delegates so chosen to deliberate (or bargain) on the nomination decision. The principle of direct democracy derived from the Progressive era, when some state legislatures intervened in the nominating process, stripping parties of their control over delegate selection and establishing state-run presidential primaries. Direct democracy found institutional expression under the mixed system in primaries in which delegates were either chosen or mandated in accordance with their expressed preference for national candidates. Delegates chosen by this method became spokesmen for the voters' choice for a national candidate and carried the voters' message to the national conventions.

Some of the institutional supports for the representative component of the mixed system began to weaken well before 1968, as long-term changes in the political system eroded the power of traditional party structures. Civil service reform on the state and local levels undermined the organizational base of many big-city machines; national welfare-state legislation removed the need for many of the parties' previous services; and a more educated and middle-class electorate grew more reluctant to follow the dictates of party bosses. In the 1950s, television began to be used in political campaigns, making it easier for individual presidential aspirants to bypass existing organizations and establish direct communication with the voters.

It was not until 1968, however, that the tensions over the nominating process erupted into a major political conflict. Meeting in the midst of growing controversy and confrontation over the Vietnam War, both political parties were under pressure to offer new ways to handle this foreign policy crisis. The Democratic party, as the era's majority party, became the focal point of this pressure, and the splits in the nation were mirrored in the divisions within the party. In Chicago, large numbers of citizens demonstrated at the site of the Democratic convention, protesting the party's decision to nominate Hubert Humphrey. Convinced that the existing nominating process was illegitimate and that a more open and democratic system would have produced an antiwar candidate, these demonstrators and their supporters throughout the nation demanded immediate institutional change.

Within the party itself, reformers echoed many of these general sentiments and succeeded in persuading the convention to adopt a vaguely worded call for party reform. The McGovern–Fraser Commission, established as a result of the convention's decision, proceeded to promulgate a bold set of national party rules regulating the delegate selection process. These rules set in motion a whole series of events taken by state legislatures and subsequent party commissions that undermined the mixed system and led to a nominating process based essentially on the principle of direct democracy. Analysts who have surveyed this period have not reached a consensus on whether these party reformers actually opposed the representative concept outright or intended "merely" to reform it, cleansing it of its irregular and undemocratic features and stripping it of any connection with traditional party organizations and leaders. But whatever their precise intentions—and the final record undoubtedly will show a mixture of motives—the results are not in question: today aspirants for party nominations present themselves directly to the voters in a series of popular or plebiscitary contests, and it is the verdicts in these contests that decide the outcomes.

An examination of the changed methods of delegate selection clearly reveals the shift. In 1968, less than half of the delegates to both party conventions were chosen in primaries, and the power over the nomination still rested in large measure with leaders of traditional party organizations; by 1980, more than three-quarters of the delegates were selected or mandated in primaries, and the voters in these contests, for all intents and purposes, chose the nominees. Other changes also have moved the process in the direction of direct democracy. In 1968, most convention delegates retained at least the theoretical option of exercising a discretionary choice; by 1980, delegates had been transformed in most instances into instructed messengers, bound to their preferences not only by state laws, but, in the case of the Democratic party, by a controversial national rule as well. The connection between delegate contests and the voters' expression of national candidate preference was strengthened by the widespread use of proportional representation, which automatically allotted delegates to national candidates, rather than allowing them to stand individually, as many primary laws formerly required. Finally, Congress enacted campaign finance legislation, which, though partly unrelated to these developments, put the federal government's implicit stamp of recognition on the democratic system.

Taken together, these changes completely transformed the environment in which presidential nominations take place. Political parties, understood as agents able to act on their own initiative, have all but ceased to exist in the nominating process. Parties may regain their strength in other areas, as the Republican party seems to have done since 1980, but this development will occur in spite of, and not because of, their role in the nominating system. The parties in the nominating process are now merely labels, which individual aspirants now vie to capture. The loss of party control over the nominating process has created a new set of incentives for presidential aspirants. Instead of attempting to make themselves acceptable to party leaders, they turn to mass politics and practice the arts of popular leadership. As a consequence, aspirants now declare their candidacies earlier than before, attempt to build mass personal organizations—in effect, temporary national parties—and then pursue the nomination by courting public constituencies. The "power" in this process is no longer in the hands of a set of power brokers acting within the confines of the institutional setting of the convention; instead, it lies in the interaction between the candidates and voters, and therefore to some extent in those structures that mediate between them—especially the news media.

These characteristics of current campaigns have become so pronounced that many now refer regularly to the existence of a new nominating system. Although accurate in one sense—for the system clearly has changed profoundly—it is potentially misleading in another, for it implies that a stable new arrangement has come into being. If past experience can serve as a guide, however, caution should be exercised before claiming that a process of institutional change has ended. In previous transformations of the nominating system, the process of change extended over many years and involved a series of adjustments and readjustments before equilibrium was finally achieved. The transformation from the congressional caucus to the convention system lasted from 1816 until 1840, while the evolution of the mixed system took from 1908 until 1924. Just as the mixed system came into being in a two-stage process of an assertion of and a reaction to the Progressive call for direct democracy, so the current criticisms of the prevailing system may indicate that we are today still in the midst of a period of change.

No matter how the system may develop in the future, it is clear that the reform impulse of the last decade has now run its course and brought most of its ideas to their logical conclusion. The next step in the process of change will require a fresh initiative and a new name — or at the very least a recognition that it is time to begin reforming the reforms. Further efforts at change need not, however, imply a complete rejection of the recent reforms or a desire to return to some mythical Golden Age. The reforms clearly changed many practices that could not be justified, whether by the standards of democratic or representative decisionmaking; and reform rules help in some areas to establish a kind of "social contract" between various groups and the political parties in regard to their access to the political system.

Although criticism of institutions by its nature often exaggerates current problems—thereby provoking a defensive reaction from the architects of the prevailing system—most discussion of the nominating process today is concerned not with settling past disputes but with laying the foundation for an improved system in the future. Current criticisms of the nominating process ask legislators to consider whether the present system has not created incentives for party discord and factionalism, produced campaigns that are too long and that sap the strength and divert the proper attention of governing authorities, and created a method that, for all its formal attributes of democracy, is subject to serious distortions of the public will by interest groups and through the effects of media coverage.

Legislators in the last decade, whatever their real inclinations may have been, operated under the constraints imposed by a false definition of the nomination problem. The events that surrounded the race for the Democratic nomination in 1968 led many opinion leaders to identify the concept of representation with all the corrupt aspects of the old politics, from irregular selection procedures to back-room bargains. Once this identification became fixed in the public's mind and in the sentiments of most political commentators, it was impossible to entertain the idea of substituting a reformed representative system for the system of the "old" politics. The only choice, it seemed, was between a (necessarily) corrupt representative system and direct democracy.

Today, however, the memories of 1968 have begun to fade, and the spirit of reform has subsided. Legislators now find that they have more leeway and can discuss openly the possibility of reinstituting representative mechanisms and restoring certain prerogatives to party leaders and elected officials. These ideas, virtually unthinkable—or at any rate unmentionable—only a few years ago, now are at the center of "respectable" debate on institutional change. This book is written to contribute to this debate and to help political leaders and the public to understand better the consequences of the current nominating process and the major alternatives that are now under consideration.

2 THE EVOLUTION OF THE NOMINATING SYSTEM, 1789-1968

Before the emergence of the current nominating process, presidential selection took place under four relatively distinct nominating systems: the original Constitutional Plan (1787-96); the Congressional Caucus (1800-16); the Pure Convention System (1832-1908); and the Mixed System (1924-68). A review of the major features of each of the previous systems will throw light on the character of the current system.

THE CONSTITUTIONAL PLAN

Because the Founding Fathers neither wanted nor expected national political parties, the original plan for presidential selection did not include a distinct partisan nominating phase. The system constructed by the Founders was predicated on and designed to foster a nonpartisan electoral process that would select the president from among illustrious national figures. The major elements of the selection process, from the winnowing of the number of candidates to the final election itself, were governed by constitutional provision, thus obviating all need (in theory) for private associations such as political parties.

Under the constitutional plan, each state was assigned a number of electors equal to the total of its senators and representatives. The state legislatures were empowered to decide how the electors would be chosen, with direct popular election and selection by the legislatures being the two methods that were most frequently contemplated. Once selected, however, the electors became national officials operating under a constitutional mandate. The Founders took every precaution at this point to ensure that the selection process would be genuinely representative and deliberative. Recognizing that the method used to choose the electors might bind their voters, the Founders gave the electors two votes, one of which almost certainly would be at the electors' discretion. Meeting in their separate states, the electors would deliberate about their choice, with some preliminary communications probably taking place among electors from different states. As the Founders envisioned this process to work in practice, electors would consider not only which candidates they preferred but also which candidate had a chance to win. The desire of each elector to have a voice in determining the outcome would supply the motive for compromise and for finding an electable candidate.

In determining the number of electoral votes required for election, the Founders sought to walk a fine line between guaranteeing that an elected president has a broad enough base of national support and providing a reasonable probability that the election could be decided by the electors. Their solution was to require that the victor have a vote total equal to at least half the number of *electors.* Since each elector had *two* votes, this requirement would not be all that difficult to meet. Under the constitutional plan, accordingly, the winnowing and electing functions normally would take place at the same time. The vice-president also would be chosen as part of this process. The runner-up in electoral votes to the president would be named vice-president, a provision that seems odd in a partisan age but that is at least understandable in a nonpartisan regime.

In the event that no individual received enough electoral votes to be elected president, or in the event of a tie between two individuals receiving more than the requisite number of votes, the election would be decided by the House of Representatives. In the first instance, the House would choose from among the top five on the electoral list, and in the second, from between the two individuals who had tied.

The constitutional procedures for election by the House involved a cumbersome method that was devised late in the Constitutional Convention and that was intended as a compromise to satisfy the demands of the smaller states. Each state was given one vote, to be decided in an unspecified manner among its representatives, and a majority of all the states was required to elect. James Madison, among others, complained of the undemocratic character of this procedure at the convention and predicted, prophetically, that it would lead to problems in the future.[1]

The Founders' selection system was designed to provide for some popular influence, but an influence mediated by the discretion of representatives. Popular responsiveness, however, was not the only or even the most important of the Founders' objectives for the presidential selection process. They were concerned also with making sure that the method of selection was consistent with the kind of presidency they wanted, that it channeled the ambitions of the potential candidates in a constructive way, and that it avoided some of the dangers of popular elections. Thus, except when the auxiliary method of election by the House was used, the system was designed to provide the president with a source of electoral support independent of the legislature, thereby supporting the basic doctrine of separation of powers. In order to have a chance of winning over the electors, aspirants would be encouraged to acquire distinguished records of public service and to avoid divisive and demagogic appeals. The Founders' system was ingenious, if somewhat cumbersome, and might have survived in something like its original form if it had not been for the rise of political parties. In failing to foresee this development, however, the Founders clearly revealed the extent to which they had overestimated the degree of consensus in American politics and underestimated the need for subsequent changes of a fundamental sort.

THE CAUCUS SYSTEM

The constitutional system in its pure form lasted for two or at the most three presidential elections. Without being officially changed, its operations nonetheless were altered dramatically by the advent of political parties during the 1790s. The parties effectively removed the "winnowing" function from the electoral system. Parties formed as private associations of citizens banding together and acting in concert to promote a common goal. Party adherents agreed to submerge their differences with respect to candidate preference and to work together for a single candidate agreed on by the association in advance of the election. In other words, the parties performed the task of nominating, in the sense that this function is now understood.

The first method that parties used to nominate derived from the only practical institutional mechanism readily at hand—meetings of the parties' membership in Congress. This device, known as the caucus, and later called "King Caucus" by its detractors, brought together an existing group of national political leaders who were relatively well acquainted with the sentiment of their constituents and knowledgeable about the qualities and personalities of the major presidential aspirants. In fact, because the members of Congress were much more a part of the national establishment than the electors, nomination by the caucuses marked in one respect a closing of the selection process to greater control by elites. Balancing this change, however, was the opportunity for the public or the state legislators to choose directly between teams of electors pledged to support one or another of the parties in the final election.

Reliance on the caucus was by no means equal between the two parties. In the case of the declining Federalist party, membership in Congress dwindled so rapidly that it soon became impractical to limit the nominating decision to the party's Washington contingent. By 1812, the party's nominating meetings therefore included important party leaders no longer holding federal office. Indeed, there is even some question about whether the party controlled the nominating function at all after 1808. In 1812, De Witt Clinton of New York threatened to run on his own without official support from the party, and the party's nominating meeting may have had no alternative but to adopt his candidacy. For the Democratic–Republican party, the caucus functioned from 1800 through 1816 and managed successfully to nominate and then elect the three candidates of the Virginia dynasty—Jefferson, Madison, and Monroe. Opposition to the caucus was strong, however, and disappointed aspirants attacked the institution, especially as the Federalist party grew weaker and ceased to offer a credible challenge.

The use of party nominations altered the original constitutional system in two interrelated ways. First, the parties took over the functions of narrowing the field of contestants and insuring for each a relatively broad national following. Second, through the parties' informal control over state legislatures and voters, they managed to bind the decisions of most of the electors. In effect, the electors now became instructed agents rather than discretionary representatives. A representative decisionmaking process in the selection of the president was now confined to the internal party processes during the nominating stage, while the final election was now effectively decided by those choosing the electors. Early in the nineteenth century, the states used a variety of methods for selecting the electors, but by 1832, all but two of the states held popular elections. In effect, the system of nomination by the political parties helped to lay the foundation for the democratic election of the president.

The new electoral system never obtained full recognition in constitutional law, although it was granted partial and implicit accommodation by the Twelfth Amendment (1804). This amendment was a result of the election crisis of 1800, in which confusion over the intended presidential and vice-presidential choices of the Democratic–Republican electors resulted in a tie between Jefferson and Burr. The Twelfth Amendment changed the electoral system in two important respects. First, it separated the votes for president and vice-president and gave the electors only one vote for each office. The requirement for election remained a majority of the electors for each office, which now, of course, meant a majority of the electoral votes. Second, in the event that the election had to be decided by the House, the House would have to choose from among the top three, instead of the top five, electoral vote recipients. This new system implicitly recognized that parties now were forming tickets for president and vice-president and that an elector's vote was probably no longer fully discretionary. The amendment did not, however, fully change the system, in that it did not accord formal recognition to parties, and the electors still maintained in principle the right to cast their vote according to their own discretion. Thus, for the most part, the new electoral system of partisan nominations was simply grafted onto the older constitutional system by means of informal amendment. This system still exists today, with the difficulties attendant on it, including the problem of the so-called faithless elector.

The caucus system in the Democratic–Republican party began to disintegrate in the election of 1820; by 1824, it was completely defunct. "Nomination" in the election of 1824 took place by self-declaration, by meetings of citizens, and by state legislatures. There were at least three reasons for the demise of the caucus system. First, its reliance on congressional representatives meant that in constituencies represented by congressmen from the opposite party, party members had no voice whatsoever in the selection of the nominee. For these persons, the nomination process was not sufficiently broad-based. Second, because the Democratic–Republican party was by far the dominant party of the era, the nomination by the congressional caucus was tantamount to election. This fact raised an important constitutional question, in that it threatened the independent base of electoral authority for the president established by the Founders to help maintain separation of powers. Likewise, with only one party, nomination by the caucus confined the effective participation in the presidential selection process to the members of Congress, since it was they who not only nominated but also in effect determined who would be elected to the presidency. Finally, and most important of all, after 1820 the original rationale that justified the system of party nominations no longer existed. The act of combining on behalf of one nominee was a step that partisans had taken in the early nineteenth century in order to maximize the election chances of an individual holding the "right" principles as viewed from a partisan perspective. That had been necessary because *both* parties engaged in the practice of nominating. After 1816, however, the Federalist party ceased to nominate or offer opposition at the presidential level. With the discipline supplied by an opposition party no longer a factor, members of the Democratic–Republican party saw no reason to continue submerging their differences on individual candidates. Indeed, most national political leaders remained opposed in principle to the use of parties and justified their existence during the period of the caucus as a temporary deviation based on an "emergency." With the demise of the Federalist party, these leaders were only too pleased to return to a nonpartisan system that operated on the correct principles of Jeffersonian political thought.

THE CONVENTION SYSTEM

The election of 1824 revealed the serious problems inherent in a nonpartisan contest under the conditions established by the Twelfth Amendment and by the practice of binding electors. Now that the electors were committed to a single choice, the electoral system under the Constitution could no longer perform a winnowing function; and with the demise of party nominating mechanisms, no non-governmental group operated to build a national coalition. The result was electoral fragmentation that inevitably meant selection by the House. Legislators in the 1820s believed that this pattern would continue unless the electors were again given discretion or parties were reestablished. Almost every politician thought that election by the House was an evil that should be avoided. As Martin Van Buren noted in 1826, "there is no point on which the people of the United States were more perfectly agreed than upon the propriety, not to say the absolute necessity, of taking the election away from the House of Representatives."[2]

Although Congress debated a variety of plans that would repeal the Twelfth Amendment and restore discretion to the electors, none was adopted. The pressures for democracy and the continuing conflicts between small and large states made electoral reform through the amendment process almost impossible. As an alternative, the advocates of political parties led by Martin Van Buren proposed the "informal" amendment of reinstituting party competition. With two major parties, this system would all but guarantee that the election was decided at the electoral stage and not in the House. Aligning himself and his followers with Andrew Jackson in the election of 1828, Van Buren managed to win Jackson to the doctrine of two-party competition, and eventually—by 1840—the doctrine became accepted as part of the operating constitution of the United States.

When parties were reestablished, however, the convention was employed as a new device for nominating presidential candidates, replacing the discredited congressional caucus. More broadly based than the caucus and better able to represent party members from every section of the country, the convention also allayed fears about congressional interference with the president's separate base of authority in the selection process. Indeed, the mere fact that the election would again be contested at the final stage assured the president of a genuine constituency beyond the Congress. In addition, the convention system marked a change in power within the political parties that transferred the decisionmaking power from members of Congress, who controlled the nominating system under the caucus system, to state and local power brokers, who tended to dominate the convention. This change represented a movement toward federalism in America's parties, since the state party organizations now became the pivotal powers in determining the choice of the president.

The nominating conventions, and indeed the political parties themselves, were self-governing entities that established their own rules of conduct, initially independent of any interference or regulation by public authorities.[3] In determining the requisite number of votes needed for nomination, the Whig party employed the usual principle of majority rule. The Democrats, however, adopted at their first convention, in 1832, a rule requiring a two-thirds majority to nominate. In the Democratic party, this rule reinforced the power of the states, or more precisely of regions, allowing any major regional bloc to prevent the nomination of a candidate it opposed. In effect, the rule implemented something akin to Calhoun's idea of the concurrent majority, according to which every major interest in the nation, in order to protect its rights, should possess a veto over the policy decisions of the government. In particular, the two-thirds rule served most often to protect the special interests of the South. Although only two candidates were ever denied the nomination after receiving a majority of the votes of the convention—Martin Van Buren in 1844 and Champ Clark in 1912—the rule affected the outcome of other races by altering the calculations of political leaders and presidential aspirants. The rule was finally eliminated at the 1936 convention, a change that helped to "nationalize" the Democratic party. Democrats, in contrast to Republicans, also permitted the unit rule in state voting, according to which the majority of a delegation, if authorized by the state party, could cast the vote of the entire delegation for a particular candidate or position. This unit rule was not banned in the Democratic party until 1972. The two-thirds and the unit rules, along with the greater ideological emphasis on states rights, undoubtedly had the effect of making the nomination decision more difficult for Democrats than for Republicans. From the advent of the convention system in 1832 until the abolition of the two-thirds rule in 1936, the Democrats held seven conventions in which more than ten ballots were needed to decide the nomination, compared with only two for the Whigs and Republicans.

In the apportionment of delegates, both parties initially allocated delegates on the basis of their electoral college vote. Before the Civil War, the Democrats and the Whigs allowed one delegate for each electoral vote. The Republican party doubled the number of delegates after the Civil War, and the Democratic party followed suit in 1872. By the election of 1912, taking into account the slight addition of representation for the territories, the conventions numbered just under 1,100 delegates, small by today's standards, but still the largest representative body in American national politics.

The practice of apportioning delegates on the basis of party strength within the states as well as electoral votes did not begin until 1916, when the Republican party reduced the representation of the southern states. The change acknowledged the sectional character of the party's following and was precipitated by the Republican disaster of 1912. In that election, Taft won the nomination from Teddy Roosevelt with strong support from the delegations of southern states. As usual, however, these states supported the Democratic candidate in the final election. Moreover, Taft finished behind Teddy Roosevelt in most northern states. (Roosevelt ran a third-party campaign as the Progressive candidate.) The healing of the party's open schism in 1916 produced the reduction in the South's voting power at the Republican convention. In 1924, the Republicans pushed this reform further, creating a "bonus" system that gave more delegates to the states in which the Republican candidate won the presidential vote in the previous election. In 1944, the Democrats adopted a similar system, in part to assuage the southern states for their loss of influence from the abolition of the two-thirds rule. Since the 1940s, both parties have changed their bonus formulas, and each party now uses different criteria for awarding bonus delegates. Both parties, moreover, have allowed dramatic increases in the number of delegates at the national conventions (see Figure 2–1). The apportionment formula of the Republican party was challenged in the courts in 1972 on the principles of one person-one vote and one party voter-one vote, but the courts reaffirmed the national party's power to set its own apportionment formula.[4]

Throughout the nineteenth century, and in fact until the reforms of the 1970s, the selection of delegates was handled almost entirely by the states, whether by the state party organizations or (after 1904) by state laws. The national parties intervened in the seating of delegates on an ad hoc basis in credentials disputes, but seldom directly dictated rules or criteria for choosing delegates.[5] The state parties in the nineteenth century used a variety of methods for selecting delegates. In some states, they were chosen all or in part by state party committees or by the governor. Most of the delegates in

Figure 2-1. Number of Delegates to the National Party Conventions, 1832-1980.

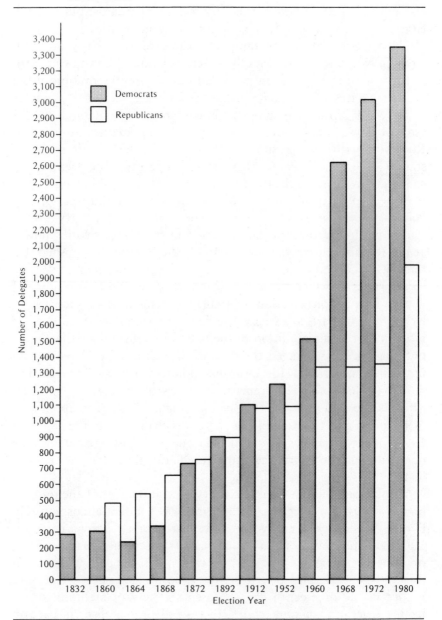

Source: Congressional Quarterly, *Guide to U.S. Elections* (1975).

most states, however, were selected by state party conventions, comprised of delegates chosen from lower level party caucuses and conventions, often in a two- or three-step process. The degree of procedural democracy in these processes varied from state to state and within each state from area to area. Most of the time, however, the selection of delegates to the state conventions and the subsequent selection of national convention delegates were controlled by the party organizations and their leaders. As a result, the tone of the national conventions reflected the varying and constantly changing character of the state and local party organizations. Sometimes the delegates were concerned primarily with ideological questions and sometimes primarily with "material" concerns, that is, finding an electable candidate willing to provide the local party with federal patronage. As the state and local parties became, on the whole, more oriented toward material concerns after the Civil War, the delegates at the national conventions likewise became more preoccupied with striking patronage bargains, a fact that gave rise to the widespread complaints that conventions were corrupt assemblies of greedy politicians.

The control over the selection of delegates exercised by party officials made it virtually impossible for presidential aspirants to influence directly the makeup of the delegations, except in their home states. Campaigning publicly for the nomination or attempting to win delegates to one's candidacy during the delegate selection process would not only have been pointless in the nineteenth century but also almost certainly counterproductive, as state and local party leaders would have resented the challenge to their prerogatives. Before the convention and the election year, the most that candidates could do in the way of "campaigning" for the nomination was to make their names known and seek to build alliances with leaders who had influence in the selection of delegates. In contrast to campaigns today, the nominating campaign began in an active sense only after the selection of the delegates and usually not until the convention itself. Aspirants then devised plans to attempt to inspire enthusiasm among the delegates and to influence the convention's coalition-building process. (According to the norms of the day, under which it was held that "the office should seek the man and not the man the office," recognized candidates seldom attended the convention, and most of the maneuvering was conducted on their behalf by supporters and key lieutenants.)

The nation's attention in presidential nominations, accordingly, was focused on the conventions and not on the delegate selection process. Although the final choice of the nominee clearly was conditioned by that process, the actual decisions usually were made at the conventions. From 1868 until 1912, eleven of the twenty-four nomination decisions were made *after* the first ballot, and of the thirteen first-ballot victories, six took place when an incumbent was renominated. Indeed, incumbents themselves were not always assured of renomination, as partisans of the day followed the adage expressed by Thomas Reed that "a good party is better than the best man that ever lived." Because the nomination was made by convention, students of presidential nominations focused chiefly on convention behavior. The convention, from most accounts, was a unique and unfathomable representative body that was small and well enough controlled to be capable of bargaining and deliberation, but still large enough on occasion to behave as a mass assembly moved by sudden shifts of sentiment—"stampedes"—that swept through the convention hall. Still, the conventions generally were marked by a cautious pragmatism that emphasized victory. As James Bryce wrote, "The task of the party convention is to choose the party candidate—who is most likely to win."[6]

THE MIXED SYSTEM

The mixed system is the name that some political scientists have given to the nominating process that emerged, unplanned, from the assault, but incomplete conquest, of Progressives on the pure convention system of the nineteenth century. By 1924, after twelve years of great change and uncertainty in the nominating process, the mixed system was firmly in place.

The Progressive movement, like most political movements, contained diverse elements, some of which were concerned simply with the practical objective of winning power. Nonetheless, the movement presented a coherent alternative theory of nomination that was at once consistent with the Progressives' immediate bid for power and the theoretical concerns of their public spokesmen. As their first objective, the Progressives sought to end the corruption of the existing political system, which was in their view primarily a result of the activities of the political parties. Next, they wanted to remove the pluralistic influence of interest groups and localistic pressures on the nominating process. And finally, in a more positive vein, the Progressives wanted to alter the American political system so that it would be more open to change originating from the national government. This last objective required a powerful president who could command public opinion and galvanize it to make the government act with greater energy.

To achieve these goals, the Progressives called for the destruction of existing sources of power within the parties and the transformation of the entire character of parties, if not their outright elimination. The cry behind which the Progressives rallied public opinion was for more democracy in the nominating process. Their institutional plan involved changing the locus of decisionmaking in the nominating process from the convention to the preconvention stage and altering the way in which aspirants competed for party nominations. Candidates would have to abandon a brokering style of bargaining with party leaders (an "inside" strategy) in favor of a popular leadership style that would appeal to public opinion and generate a popular constituency during the campaign (an "outside" strategy). Structurally, the Progressives intended to accomplish these changes by converting the nominating process from its existing status as a "privately" controlled associational activity to a state-run public function, ideally through a national primary, but failing that, through a system of delegate selection primaries enacted by the individual states. Under this scheme, the parties would be partly incorporated into the official constitution and regulated more closely. The plan would bring the nominating process under the control of public authority, as the Founders had originally wanted, but with the very opposite objective: making the system wholly democratic instead of representative.

The national primary concept was endorsed in the Progressive party platform of 1912 and was proposed by President Woodrow Wilson in his first annual message to Congress (1913); Congress was not receptive. The alternative state primary movement sanctioned by the Democratic party in its platform of 1912, however, made great strides during the Progressive era. Four states had some type of presidential primary law by 1908, fifteen by 1912, and twenty-six by 1916, the highpoint of primary legislation until 1976. After 1916, the number began to drop off, falling to twenty-one in 1920 and to sixteen by 1936.

Despite the large number of states with primary laws during the second decade of this century, the Progressives for a number of reasons failed to make competition in the primaries the dominant element in determining the outcome of the nomination process. In the critical test year of 1916, when the primary route to the nomination had the best chance of being established, the Democrats had a popular incumbent, Woodrow Wilson, and as a result, the race was virtually uncontested. On the Republican side, no truly popular candidate entered the primaries and captured the nation's imagination; this allowed the convention to nominate Charles Evan Hughes, a Supreme Court Justice who never campaigned publicly for the nomination and who was officially entered (without filing himself) in only one primary. Among the other reasons for the failure of the primary movement were the nature of the primary laws and existing party rules; the laws governing primaries were complicated, involving early filing dates and high petition requirements. In some states, delegates were not legally committed by the primaries. Moreover, the Democrats still had their two-thirds rule in effect, making it impossible for any Democratic aspirant to win nearly enough delegates to capture the nomination.

None of the candidates employing an active outside strategy in 1916 or in 1920 succeeded in winning their party's nomination, and by 1924, the major aspirants seemed to have learned from experience that an outside strategy was not by itself sufficient. For quite some time thereafter, the major candidates did not use this approach as the major element of their campaigns, although many candidates entered selected primaries, often without publicly campaigning. Indeed, after 1920, even the theoretical prospect of capturing the nomination by a pure outside strategy diminished as structural retrenchments from the Progressive reforms began to take place. These assumed at least three different forms: the outright repeal of primary laws; the de facto insulation of the primaries from national focus through laws that barred delegates from specifying on the ballot which candidate they preferred; and the development of a tradition in some states, enforced by the power of the state parties, of running favorite sons in the primaries.

Before examining the characteristics of the mixed system that emerged after 1924, it is interesting to speculate on the possible parallels between the events of the Progressive period and those that have been taking place since 1968. The Progressive period, like the reform era that began in 1968, opened with a burst of democratic changes and a rush to primary legislation by the states. Yet by 1920, a number of states, acting without fanfare or loud declarations of principle, had altered or repealed the Progressive innovations, returning some, though not all, of the decisionmaking power to the state party organizations. Today, some of those who wish to see a resurgence of representative decisionmaking wonder if the same kind of change occurring in the same way could take place in the years ahead.

It is clear that today, as in the 1920s, the enthusiasm for direct democracy has diminished greatly among political leaders since the early days of reform. Our politicians no longer feel obligated to sing the same praises of "openness" or to offer democratic procedures as the panacea for every institutional problem. Moreover, in an occurrence similar to what took place in 1916 and 1920, some primaries in 1980 experienced such low turnout rates that many citizens in these states have begun to question whether holding a primary is worthwhile. In Kansas, for example, 27 percent of the electorate voted in the presidential primary in 1980, in Alabama 17 percent, and in Louisiana just 15 percent—hardly levels of participation that inspire great confidence in claims of democratic decisionmaking.

There are, however, some very significant differences between the situation today and that at the close of the Progressive era. First, the modification of primary laws aimed at insulating delegates from national races was a matter entirely under the authority of the state legislatures in the 1920s, whereas today, at least in the case of the Democratic party, the national party has established a series of detailed rules governing the character of all delegate selection processes. Second, the decline in enthusiasm for primaries at the end of the Progressive era resulted in part from the movement's failure to establish the primary route as the dominant element in the nomination contest. Today, primaries already have become the key component to the nomination decision. Third, state parties in the 1920s were probably stronger than they are today and therefore better able to reassert their power once the enthusiasm for democratic forms had waned. Finally, the alternative to the primaries in the 1920s was, in most states, a caucus system over which the party organization could exercise a controlling influence. Today, under national Democratic party rules and under a different balance between primaries and caucuses, there is much uncertainty, as we shall see, about which groups or elements in the nation would gain from a return to caucus procedures.

Any parallel between the end of the Progressive era and the current period is therefore imperfect, at best. Granted there may be some factors operating today, as after 1920, that could result in movement toward representative decisionmaking in the nominating process by the simple means of state and state party action. Nevertheless, it seems clear that the degree of interference that has already come from authorities above the state level and the degree to which the democratic system has established itself have changed the situation greatly. Today, a return to representative decisionmaking undoubtedly would require a more conscious national effort and some kind of coordinated plan from either the Congress or the national parties, even if that "plan" were to be as minimal as that of returning certain powers to the states and state parties.

The mixed system that emerged in 1924 rested on an uneasy balance between progressive notions of presidential selection and the ideas of those who helped to establish partisan competition in the 1820s. During the period in which the mixed system was in existence, those who sought the presidency had the option of following a purely inside strategy of dealing with party leaders and delegates after they were chosen or of choosing a modified outside strategy of competing in primaries and attempting to force themselves on the party leaders. The system also produced a blend of these two strategies in which a candidate entered some primaries to win delegates and demonstrate popular appeal while at the same time carrying on negotiations with party leaders and avoiding where possible any outright challenge to their power. Naturally, the strategy that candidates adopted had a great deal to do with their situation and their assessment of their own strengths and weaknesses; a candidate like Estes Kefauver, who had little support among party regulars, could try only the outside route, while Lyndon Johnson in 1960, weighed down by the responsibilities of being Majority Leader in the Senate and lacking broader popular appeal outside his home region, chose the inside route. In addition, changes in the political environment of the nominating system, such as the advent of television, had the effect, toward the end of the period, of increasing the importance of primaries.

Convention behavior under the mixed system was somewhat different than under the pure convention system of the nineteenth century. Party leaders had the dominant say in both cases, but under the mixed system their influence was subject to more checks and constraints. The primaries provided a significant minority of bound delegates and gave tangible evidence of a candidate's popular appeal. Public opinion was therefore a consideration that party leaders were now almost obliged to take into account. Still, the conventions retained a good deal of discretion and were not bound to follow the popular mandate as expressed in the primaries, as illustrated by the Republican's choice of Willkie over Dewey in 1940 and of Stevenson over Kefauver in 1952. Indeed, because many contenders did not enter the primaries, primary election results could not establish unequivocally which candidate was the popular favorite. In fact, if responsiveness to the wishes of the rank and file is one criterion by which conventions are judged, the conventions under the mixed system were highly responsive. Using poll data rather than primary results, two scholars calculated that in the period from 1936 through 1968 the conventions denied the popular favorite the nomination in only one clear-cut case—in 1952, when Adlai Stevenson trailed far behind Estes Kefauver in the polls but won the nomination. In two other cases, the correspondence between the "winner" in the poll results and the winner of the nomination were ambiguous or too close to call—in 1940, when Wendell Willkie was closing quickly on Thomas Dewey and overtook him in a poll taken after the convention began, and in 1964, when there was a virtual dead heat in the polls among Barry Goldwater, Richard Nixon, Henry Cabot Lodge, Jr., and William Scranton.[7]

Poll results are, of course, greatly influenced by the character of the prevailing nominating system. During the period of the mixed system, at least until 1956, it was accepted practice for aspirants *not* to enter all the primaries, and people's preference for the nominee was almost certainly more independent of the candidate's performance in the primaries than it is today. (Currently, because everyone realizes that the chances of being nominated are determined by performance in the primaries, public opinion is influenced more heavily by what occurs in these contests.) Whether poll results independent of primary performance offered a better indication of genuine popular sentiment than poll results that reflect primary performance is a question that could be endlessly debated. In any case, the fact that the conventions of the mixed period regularly selected the rank-and-file favorite, even when that candidate did not participate in the primaries, indicated the importance of popular support to party leaders of that era. Nor should this "democratic" result be surprising. One of the two major justifications of a representative process is precisely that it is better suited than an electoral process to determine the popular choice, in that it can account for evidence not always revealed in elections. The other justification for representation, which might fit the case of the Democratic convention of 1952, is that a representative assembly, even when it knows the popular favorite, can choose to exercise its own discretion on behalf of such considerations as the qualifications of the candidates or their chances of being elected in the general election.

The character of an institutional system, it must be emphasized, is a function not only of the rules and laws that directly govern its arrangement but also of environmental factors, such as evolving practices, shifting norms, and technological developments. These environmental factors combined in the latter years of the mixed system to produce two incremental changes. The first was an increased reliance on the primaries by aspirants after 1948. Although many candidates still employed an inside strategy—Stevenson in 1952, Johnson in 1960, and Humphrey in 1968—scholars of the process often noted the increasing pressures to enter primaries.[8] Indeed, by 1968, Humphrey's failure to participate in any primaries caused many to view his nomination as illegitimate. Evidently, as candidates made greater use of the primaries, more and more people came to expect them to use this method. Changes in the nature of the media also had an impact. By 1960, Americans began to follow nominating campaigns on television, thus allowing the individual candidate competing in the primaries to build up more pressure, when successful, on behalf of his candidacy. Television, according to Michael Robinson, helped to "deny the parties their most important function—the right to recruit and campaign for office-seekers . . . and began taking away from the parties their role as a major source of information about local or national campaigns and politics. . . ."[9]

Second, after 1952, the party conventions became less deliberative. From 1956 through 1968, no convention took more than one ballot to make its choice. (Indeed, extending the record to the present time, we have now had seven consecutive elections without a multiballoted convention—by far the longest such string since the advent of the nominating convention.) By contrast, in the period from 1920 to 1948, there were seven conventions that lasted more than one ballot, a more striking figure when one considers that only twelve conventions during this period did not involve the renomination of an incumbent.

Although the advent of the period of single-ballot conventions in 1952 marked a shift in the character of the mixed system, the scope of that change has often been exaggerated. It clearly did not mean that the conventions had completely lost their discretion. Indeed, it is only with the aid of hindsight that all the conventions between 1952 and 1968 can be called "over" before they met. Certainly they did not always appear that way to the participants or to the leading analysts of the era. Because delegates retained their capacity for discretion through the 1960s, the chance for a surprise decision could not be discounted. The last-minute movements on behalf of Stevenson at the 1960 Democratic Convention and Reagan at the 1968 Republican Convention were at the time more than mere talk.

More importantly, it is necessary to distinguish between a representative decisionmaking process and a decision made at the convention, for it does not follow that all first-ballot victors are evidence of an absence of discretionary decisionmaking. In the Democratic party nomination decisions of 1960 and 1968, for example, delegates and party leaders were reaching decisions in the preconvention period, and a great deal of bargaining and many exchanges of information took place. Given the advances in modern communications, one would hardly expect otherwise. There remains, accordingly, a great deal of difference between a nominating process in which the delegates have discretion—even if they do not exercise it *at* the convention itself—and one in which delegates are bound from the moment they are chosen. The fundamental change in the character of the nominating process in recent times, therefore, was the result of the legal and institutional changes of the reform era and not of secular trends that took place during the period of the mixed system.

3 THE REFORM ERA

The modern reform era began at the 1968 Democratic convention in Chicago. Like the Progressive movement some half-century earlier, it comprised various political forces and groups having somewhat different objectives. For many years—as was the case in the Progressive era—the chief goal was to win power, and arguments about institutional arrangements were advanced merely as weapons in a struggle for political advantage. Nonetheless, the movement had a theoretical center—no matter what the various reasons for its adoption were. Like the Progressives, modern reformers sought to weaken the power of traditional party leaders, to reduce the influence of interest groups, and to increase the amount of rank-and-file participation in the nominating process.

There is some question about how eager the reformers were to transform the nomination process into a plebiscitary decision made in the primaries. At the 1968 convention, delegates explicitly called for complete direct democracy and for a national primary. Many of those who sat on the various party reform commissions, however, sought to open the caucus states to more participation as an alternative to more primaries.[1] Nonetheless, these reformers, like the simple direct democracy advocates, lent their weight and prestige to the principle of democracy, and whether or not all of the consequences of their decisions were strictly intended, they represent a logical result of the ideas that were set in motion at the outset of the reform era.

RULES OF DELEGATE SELECTION

There were three basic changes in the delegate selection process during the reform period. First, the number of states holding primaries that either choose or bind delegates has nearly doubled since 1968. (Under this definition of primaries, the "beauty contest" preference polls that neither choose delegates nor bind the votes of delegates selected by other means are ignored.) Second, the character of the overall primary component has been altered, with a much higher percentage of delegates being chosen under rules that encourage or require them to be committed to national candidates. Finally, the caucus states, having been reduced from thirty-three in 1968 to some seventeen in 1980, have become more open to rank-and-file participation and more oriented to the selection of delegates bound to national candidates, especially in the Democratic party.

Primaries

Table 3-1 shows the dramatic growth in the number of primaries since 1968 and in the percentage of delegates chosen in primaries. From a base of under 40 percent in 1968, the number rose to over 70 percent in both parties in 1976 and 1980. But these numbers tell only part of the story. During the period of the mixed system, many of the primary states were wholly or partially insulated from choosing delegates bound to a national candidate. One method employed was the running of "favorite sons," which often prevented national candidates from entering primaries in states that had powerful party organizations or popular state figures. By the 1970s, this method, the use of which had already been declining, died out almost completely. National candidates today can enter any primary state without needing a pretext for intruding on the forbidden territory of a powerful state leader. Indeed, under the legal requirements of most primary laws today, the national candidates automatically are placed on the ballot by a state election committee or by the secretaries of state,

Table 3-1. Presidential Primaries, 1968-80.

	1968	1972	1976	1980
Democratic Party				
Number of states using a primary for selecting or binding national delegates	17	23	29	29
Number of votes cast by delegates chosen or bound by primaries	983	1862	2183	2378
Percentage of all votes cast by delegates chosen or bound by primaries	37.5	60.5	72.6	71.4
Republican Party				
Number of states using a primary for selecting or binding national delegates	16	22	28	33
Number of votes cast by delegates chosen or bound by primaries	458	710	1533	1515
Percentage of all votes cast by delegates chosen or bound by primaries	34.3	52.7	67.9	76.0

Source: Computed from figures supplied in *Congressional Quarterly Weekly Reports* (July 12, 1980; August 9, 1980); Congressional Quarterly, *Guide to U.S. Elections* (1975); *Congressional Quarterly Almanac* (1976), pp. 848, 894.

placing the onus on the candidate to withdraw from the competition. In addition, with most primary states now using proportional representation in the allocation of delegates, candidates are reluctant to pass up any opportunity to pick up at least a small share of delegates.

A second method that states formerly employed to insulate delegates in primaries from a national candidate focus was a legal ban on the listing of the delegates' candidate preference. This device had the effect of isolating the election of delegates from the national race and, in most cases, ensuring their discretion. The party organizations usually dominated such contests, and the delegates they preferred usually were selected. National Democratic party rules since 1976 have disallowed the selection of delegates from this kind of primary, and the party now has managed to achieve complete compliance on this point. The Republican party has no such rule, and in four states in 1980—Illinois, Mississippi, New York, and Pennsylvania—contests without candidate identification were permitted (see Table 3-2).

Table 3-2. Delegate Selection Methods, 1980.

	Republican	Democrat
I. Selection of delegates by caucuses	Alaska, Arizona, Arkansas, Colorado, Delaware, Hawaii, Iowa, Maine, Minnesota, Missouri, Montana, North Dakota, Oklahoma, Utah, Vermont[a] Virginia, Washington, Wyoming	Alaska, Arizona, Colorado, Delaware, Hawaii, Idaho, Iowa, Maine, Michigan, Minnesota, Mississippi, Missouri, North Dakota, Oklahoma, South Carolina, Texas, Utah, Vermont, Virginia, Washington, Wyoming
II. Selection of delegates by primary		
A. Selection of individual delegates		
1. Without candidate preference listed on ballot	Illinois, New York, Pennsylvania	
2. With candidate preference listed on ballot	District of Columbia, Mississippi, Nebraska, New Jersey, Ohio, West Virginia	Illinois, West Virginia
B. Selection or mandating of delegates according to candidate preferences		
1. Winner-take-all statewide only	California, Puerto Rico, Vermont[a]	

| 2. Winner-take-all districts and statewide | Florida, Georgia, Indiana, Louisiana,[b] Maryland, South Carolina, Texas,[c] Wisconsin | Alabama, Arkansas, California, Connecticut, District of Columbia, Florida, Georgia, Indiana, Kansas, Kentucky, Louisiana, Maryland, Massachusetts, Montana, Nebraska, Nevada, New Hampshire, New Jersey, New Mexico, New York, North Carolina, Ohio, Oregon, Pennsylvania, Puerto Rico, Rhode Island, South Dakota, Tennessee, Wisconsin |
| 3. Proportional representation | Alabama, Connecticut, Idaho, Kansas, Kentucky, Louisiana, Massachusetts, Michigan, Nevada, New Hampshire, New Mexico, North Carolina, Oregon, Rhode Island, Tennessee, Texas[c] | |

a. In Vermont on the Republican side, ten of the nineteen delegates were permitted to be bound to candidates who won the preference primary by more than 40 percent; the other nine were chosen by caucuses.

b. In Louisiana on the Republican side, the district delegates are selected on a winner-take-all basis and the statewide delegates on a proportional basis.

c. In Texas on the Republican side, the delegates are awarded on a winner-take-all basis on a district or statewide level *if* a candidate received more than 50 percent of the vote; if no candidate wins 50 percent, the delegates are awarded proportionally.

Source: Congressional Quarterly, *Guide to U.S. Elections* (1976); Congressional Quarterly, *Guide to Current American Government* (1980); *Congressional Quarterly Weekly Reports* (January–August 1980).

A final method formerly used by the states to provide some insulation of the delegates was the election of delegates as individuals with their candidate preference (including uncommitted) listed on the ballot. This kind of primary provided only a very slight degree of insulation, since most voters selected delegates on the basis of their preferred national candidate. In practice, accordingly, these contests, which were usually in multimember districts, turned out to be de facto winner-take-all races within each district because citizens tended to use all of their votes to choose delegates supporting the same candidate. Nevertheless, none of the delegates selected in these primaries was legally bound to vote for his stated candidate preference, and there were numerous instances in which voters split their choices among delegates preferring different candidates, indicating that at least some consideration was being given to the delegates' personal qualifications, irrespective of the candidates they were pledged to support. This tendency of voters to consider the delegates as individuals encouraged the slating of delegates having some prominence in their own right, and it is no surprise, therefore, that in 1976 a higher percentage of Democratic party officials was chosen under this type of primary than under either the caucus method or the candidate preference primary.[2]

As recently as 1976, most of the delegates elected by primaries in both the Democratic and the Republican parties were chosen by this method. Under Democratic party rules for 1980, however, this kind of primary was banned, and all primaries must now be *candidate* preference primaries in which voters indicate their preference not directly for each individual delegate, but for a candidate or a slate of delegates pledged to a candidate.[3] The delegates are then allocated proportionally according to the share of the votes in the constituency received by each candidate. Although the proportional requirement holds only for the Democratic party, many states have applied this method of allocating delegates to the Republican party as well. This change usually occurred when predominantly Democratic state legislatures rewrote their state laws to satisfy the national Democratic party rules and included the Republican primaries under the same general legislation. The Republican national party, however, has no rule banning winner-take-all candidate preference primaries, and in 1980, several states held such contests at the state or congressional district levels for the Republican party. (See categories II B 1 and II B 2 in Table 3–2.) Because of the differences in national party rules, states often permit the parties to conduct different kinds of primaries (see Table 3-3). The Democratic party's ban on the election of individual delegates was less the result of a determined frontal assault on the concept of individual representation than a by-product of the party's commitment to "fairness," which over the course of the 1970s led to the requirement of proportional representation. Fairness, as that concept evolved in the Democratic party's reform commissions, meant a fair reflection of the *candidate preference* of the voters and caucus participants. As this concept took hold, the selection of any delegate as an *individual* was considered unfair, for in effect it constituted a winner-take-all election, even in a constituency that chose only one delegate. By this criterion, the only fair method was a proportional allocation of delegates, and the moment that the principle of proportionality is accepted, it follows that the allocation of representatives must be made in reference to a common unit, which in this case was the candidate preference of the voters. Proportional representation has had its greatest effect thus far not in the way that it has divided delegates among the candidates but rather in forcing most delegates to be committed to a particular candidate. Under current proportional rules, the delegates become bound messengers obliged to cast their votes for the candidates, except in those few instances in which voters choose "uncommitted" as their candidate preference and manage to elect delegates so pledged.

As a method of allocating committed delegates, proportional representation obviously has a very different effect than plurality, winner-take-all contests because it awards delegate shares to candidates receiving only a small percentage of the votes. The resulting tendency to disperse the delegates among a larger number of candidates in a multicandidate race led a number of analysts to predict in 1976 that proportional representation probably would produce conventions lasting more than one ballot. Minor candidates, it was argued, would win a significant number of delegates and then would stay in the race and bargain their delegates at the convention. So far, however, this result has not materialized, and a number of factors make it unlikely that it will. First, current proportional rules allow for a cut-off figure below which a candidate receives no delegates. The cut-off level was raised between 1976 and 1980 by Democratic party rules and now, depending on the number of delegates elected in a constituency, ranges from between 15 and 25 percent, which considerably reduces the tendency toward fragmentation.[4] Second, the great likelihood

Table 3-3. Party Rules for Delegate Selection.

Party Rules—With a Difference
(major differences between national Republican and Democratic party delegate selection rules)

Issue	Democratic Party Rule	Republican Party Rule
Proportional representation	Required at all levels of the delegate selection process.	Winner-take-all permitted at the statewide and multidelegate district level.
Open or crossover primaries	Prohibited.	Prohibited unless mandated by state law.
Apportionment of delegates within a state	A complex formula is used for allocating 75 percent of a state's delegation by district. The rest are to be at large and chosen to satisfy the state's affirmative action goals and to give elected officials and state party leaders at least 10 percent of the delegation.	As determined by the state Republican committee. The rules expressly permit entire delegations to be chosen at large.
Affirmative action	State delegate selection plans must include numerical goals, timetables, and specific "outreach" activities. The "goals" are not to be "quotas," except for women, who must make up half the delegation.	"Positive action" is required, but without specific goals, timetables, or plans.
Unit rule	No delegate may be required to cast a vote in accordance with a majority at any level of the delegate selection process.	The unit rule is prohibited only for convention voting on presidential and vice-presidential nominations.

Bound delegates	All delegates are bound for one ballot unless released in writing or chosen as uncommitted delegates.	States enforce their own requirements.
Candidate preferences	Pledged delegates must be chosen from a pool of delegates publicly committed to the candidate, who may disavow any delegate.	No comparable rule.
Timing	Delegates must be chosen between the second Tuesday in March and the second Tuesday in June. Exceptions may be made for states with earlier or later procedures in 1976 if required by state law.	No specific dates are mentioned. Delegates must be chosen after the call of the convention is published and up to twenty-five days before the convention.
Compliance review	A state party whose delegate selection procedures have been approved by the party's Compliance Review Commission may be challenged at the convention only for failure to implement an approved plan.	The relative scarcity of national rules leaves little ground for a credentials challenge. But once a challenge is made, no rule grants a state any presumption that it is in compliance.
State laws	Party rules supersede state law. Where the two are in conflict, state parties may be granted exceptions if they have taken "provable positive steps" to have the law changed. No exceptions may be made for states with open primaries.	Deference to state law is written into the party rules.

Source: *National Journal* (Oct. 20, 1979), p. 1743.

that delegates will now be committed to a candidate, which itself is partly a consequence of the shift to proportional representation, has reduced the number of uncommitted delegates, thus removing the chief factor that once tended to promote a bargained nomination decision. Major candidates now compete in almost every primary and win some committed delegates even when they lose the plurality race. Finally, the proportional rule is but one rule in an entire nominating system, and many of the other rules and the dynamic of the campaign itself, including media coverage and financing, tend to narrow the field and produce a winner during the delegate selection phase. Proportional representation, while having the dispersing effect that many predicted, has been overshadowed on this count by the tendencies set in motion by other aspects of the system.

If, however, a multiballoted convention ever should occur, and if participants begin to anticipate this result as a regular possibility, proportional representation probably will change dramatically the character of the conventions. Various constituency groups—labor unions, minority groups, antiabortion forces, and the like—no doubt would attempt to win delegate support at the convention, either by running uncommitted slates or by backing single-issue candidates, as the antiabortion forces did in 1976 with Ellen McCormick. Conventions would then consist of delegates from either constituency or candidate blocs, and these two types of groups would control the choice of the nominee. The danger of such conventions is that the nominee would owe too much to one or more of the constituency groups. Formerly, the representation of these groups was to some extent mediated through the party organizations, which provided these groups with access but which also created a buffer between the nominee and the groups. In the future, these groups would be directly represented—an outcome that would stand in direct conflict with the reformers' original goal of reducing the power of interest groups.[5] In fact, the decline of party control of the convention and the "infiltration" of various pressure groups within the candidate blocs have already dramatically changed the deliberative character of the conventions: On the platform, which remains subject to the approval of the conventions, groups attempt to include their favorite policy proposals, often to the embarrassment of the nominee. The platforms, which were once pragmatic documents meant to appeal broadly to the electorate, now frequently contain the extreme positions of one or another of these pressure groups.

There is one final point about the legal status of presidential primaries that deserves mention. Primaries can be classified not only by how the delegates are chosen (as has been done so far) but also according to who is permitted to vote. The distinction usually drawn here is that between closed and open primaries. In the strict sense, an open primary is one in which any citizen may vote in either primary regardless of party affiliation, and a closed primary is one in which the voter, usually prior to the primary, must make some kind of official declaration of party affiliation for the party in whose primary that voter wishes to participate.

Prior to the reforms, the type of primary law that a state adopted was entirely its own affair. The Republican national party has made no change in this area, but the national Democratic party has adopted numerous requirements. Under current rules, open primaries in the sense defined above are no longer permitted. If a state law provides for an open primary, the national party will require its state party to choose delegates under caucus procedures. In 1980, the Democratic party in Michigan had to select its delegates by caucus for just this reason. The state of Wisconsin, which has a long tradition of an open primary, was given an exemption, as it had been in 1976. The state took its claim to the Supreme Court in 1981, arguing that the national party cannot refuse to seat delegates chosen pursuant to valid state law. The state's claim was denied in the case of *State of Wisconsin* v. *Democratic National Committee.*

Under current rules, it is unlikely that we will see very many, if any, pure open primaries. Many of the closed primaries, however, are all but open in their effects, and it is clear that for practical purposes the strict definition offered above is drawn too narrowly. Under the rubric of closed primaries, there are laws that require voters to be officially registered *before* the election in the party in whose primary they wish to participate, which have some effect in restricting crossover voting, and laws that allow the voter to change party registration at the primary election itself or merely to declare an intention to support the party's eventual nominee.[6] Because these last requirements impose little if any restriction on the voters' ability to cross over and vote in whichever primary they choose, the states that employ such rules for all intents and purposes have open primaries. By common agreement today, these states are now classified as open or crossover primaries, and in 1980, *Congressional Quarterly* listed nineteen state primaries in this category.[7]

Caucus States

During the period of the mixed nominating system, the nonprimary methods of delegate selection tended to be those in which the established party organizations exercised the greatest control. Still, these selection procedures did not preclude substantial participation by the rank-and-file members, as in the 1952 Taft–Eisenhower contest.[8] Nor did they prevent "new blood" from entering the parties and assuming control, as clearly occurred in many state parties in 1964, when conservatives loyal to Barry Goldwater took over the party machinery. Yet for the most part, the rules and norms of conduct in caucus states were strongly biased in favor of party regulars. The McGovern–Fraser Commission, a reform commission appointed pursuant to a resolution passed by the Democratic party convention of 1968, reported practices in some caucus states that, by any standards, made a mockery of any broad-based system of delegate selection. In some caucus states, delegates were chosen in the absence of any formal rules, while in others the rules were changed after the initial selection of the delegates to alter the results. In Virginia in 1968, "mass" meetings were convened in some instances on buses on the way to the state conventions. The list of abuses cited could go on and on.[9]

It is important, however, to distinguish between bona fide procedural abuses and practices that promoted a different concept of the nominating process than the democratic, candidate-oriented theory espoused by many of the reformers. For example, the McGovern–Fraser Commission report indignantly includes as an abuse the selection of delegates in some caucus states before the election year:

> More than a third of the Convention delegates [for the 1968 convention] had, in effect, already been selected prior to 1968—before either the major issues or the possible candidates were known. By the time President Johnson announced his withdrawal from the nominating contest, the delegate selection process had begun in all but twelve states.[10]

The abuse here, it should be noted, is not the existence of any procedural irregularities but rather that the party caucuses chose the delegates before the campaign had begun and the candidates had declared. Obviously, this practice would tend to help party regulars; however, if the objective is representative discretion by delegates likely to take the party's interest into account, then this system is eminently logical.

The Democratic party reforms dramatically altered the character of the caucuses. National party legislation came in two steps. The first step, taken by the McGovern–Fraser Commission for the 1972 election, banned the appointment of any ex officio delegates or the selection of any delegates by the state committees, and it instituted numerous procedural requirements, such as the preparation and dissemination of written rules, the publication of the dates of mass meetings, the holding of the meetings in the same year as the election, and the designation of a single date throughout the state for the mass meetings. These new national party rules served to facilitate access by the rank and file and, at least in 1972, reduced the influence of party organizations. The rules at this point, however, did not yet introduce any formal requirements changing the representational role of the delegates. In most states, party rules called for plurality elections of individual delegates who were not formally bound to any candidate, although quite often informal slatemaking took place, and state parties adopted their own rules or resolutions binding delegates.

The second step, taken in time for the 1976 nomination by the Mikuski Commission, applied the requirement of proportional representation to the caucus states. In so doing, it altered the character of the caucus selection process by facilitating a candidate focus in the representational role of the delegates. In this respect at least, the caucus procedures in the Democratic party produce much the same result as candidate preference primaries. Delegates are chosen not to act on behalf of the voters (except where uncommitted delegates are selected) but to register a specific candidate preference.

In practice, of course, there remain important differences between Democratic caucuses and the primaries. The number of persons who participate in the caucuses is much lower than the number who vote in primaries—in 1976, about ten times lower; and caucus meetings, unlike primaries, still involve some face-to-face contact among individuals, even if the participants no longer are involved in protracted bargaining of the sort that prevailed under plurality rules. (When plurality rules were in effect, supporters of various candidates along with various uncommitted participants frequently negotiated coalitions in an effort to secure a plurality and stop a common foe; under proportional rules, most of this bargaining is obviated, as delegate shares are assigned automatically.)

The winners and losers under these new arrangements have not always been clear, although party organizations obviously have suffered a significant diminution of their influence. In 1972, many groups opposing the Vietnam War packed the caucuses and chose delegates sympathetic to Senator McGovern, often in states where the mass of Democratic voters opposed his candidacy. This experience led a number of moderate party leaders to oppose the caucus method, fearing in particular the intrusion of these so-called amateurs or purists into state party business, which was frequently conducted at the same meetings. Paradoxically, then, some party leaders supported primaries after 1972, banking on the people to save the party from the purists. In 1976, a year without the same kind of "movement" politics afoot in the nation, the Democratic caucus results were quite different. Party regulars, often running initially as uncommitted delegates, were highly influential in a number of states, competing with and managing to limit the influence of the candidate organizations. Various organized groups, like certain labor unions, also became quite active, working either with the parties or on behalf of certain candidates. In 1980, activity by such groups, especially the National Educational Association on behalf of President Carter, was widely reported, and party regulars again made their influence felt. Few caucus delegates in 1980, however, were uncommitted, although this may have been because the contest in 1980 was a clear-cut choice between the incumbent and a single challenger.

In many states, Republican party caucuses are very different from those in the Democratic party. Because the Republican party has no national requirement for proportional representation and in fact very few national rules of any kind, they have a great deal of discretion in drawing up their delegate selection procedures. One finds, accordingly, a wide range of variation among Republican caucus plans. In Arizona, for example, the Republicans did not hold mass meetings in 1980 but restricted this stage of the process to party officials. In other states, like Minnesota, Republicans, unlike Democrats, allow independents and even Democrats to participate in their mass meetings. As a general rule, Republican caucus states elect their delegates as individuals and do not require either the caucus participants or the candidates for delegate to specify a candidate preference. In practice, the procedure leads to many winner-take-all contests, as participants vote for slates arranged "informally" by the candidate organizations. Still, as with the delegate selection primaries, many participants will consider the individual who is running as delegate as well as the candidate preference; and the fact that delegates in most states are officially uncommitted means that, whatever informal arrangements are worked out, delegates still retain the discretion to vote as they wish. At the 1976 Republican convention, there was some shifting among informally "committed" delegates up until the convention itself.

For both parties, the character of delegate selection in the caucus states cannot be treated in isolation from the developments that have taken place in the nominating process as a whole. Caucus states are no longer immune from the intrusion of the national campaigns as they often were when the majority of delegates were chosen in caucuses and when the tone of the campaign was set by the caucuses rather than by the primaries. Candidate organizations are intimately involved in the caucus races, attempting to win committed delegates. The candidates, moreover, often campaign in these states; and because caucus states have smaller turnouts than primaries, the candidates' time often can be a more important resource than money. As the first of the delegate selection contests, Iowa has received, in particular during the last two elections, more of the candidates' time than practically any other state.[11]

Generalizing about the character of caucuses today is difficult because so many changes have taken place in the last few years and because each party operates under different rules. The following statements, however, seem to constitute a reasonable summary of the current situation:

1. In "normal" election years—that is, years without large mass movements—caucus procedures are somewhat more likely than primaries to be influenced by the views and interests of the party organizations. This fact had led to the selection of more uncommitted delegates in caucuses than primaries, although, increasingly, it seems that the pressure in caucus states is to work on behalf of a national candidate.

2. National candidate organizations are now very active in caucus states and carry out most of the usual campaign activities, including advertising and organizing of local volunteers. To a significant degree, these organizations influence the results of the caucus procedures, sometimes working with party leaders.

3. Organized interest groups—for example, unions, right-to-life groups, and so forth—have been very active, working usually on behalf of one of the candidates. In return, these groups expect the support of the candidates for the position and the right to name delegates to the national convention, often to indicate the group's strength and to promote its interests during the writing of the platform.

Party Centralization of the Delegate Selection Process

Prior to the reforms, almost all the delegate selection rules were controlled either by the states or by the state parties. Since 1972, the national Democratic party has preempted much of this authority, thus assuming a new power of "legislating" the character of the delegate selection process. Although the Republican party theoretically possesses the same authority, it thus far has adopted most of its rules with a view to respecting the sovereignty of the states and state parties. Despite the Republican national party's reluctance to get involved in national rulemaking, Republican delegate selection rules were changed in many states, usually when legislatures took action in response to Democratic party rules and included Republicans under the same legislation. Thus, Republican selection procedures frequently have been written along the lines established by the national Democratic party because the Democrats had control of many state governments during the decade.

The new power of the Democratic national party—and by implication of both national parties—is certainly one of the most important institutional changes of the reform era. But this power is not without limits, practical or legal, which must be clearly understood. The Democratic national party's power in the case of state *party* rules is nearly plenary. Through its procedures for reviewing state party plans, the national party has carefully scrutinized delegate selection procedures in caucus states and has ordered these states to make changes where necessary. In the case of state laws, the Democratic party's claim is not, strictly speaking, that the national party has the authority to tell the states what laws to pass. All that the party claims is the power to determine which delegates shall be seated at its own convention. Its power to legislate in the case of state law is therefore indirect. If a state has a primary law that conflicts with party rules, the national party may make it clear that it will not seat these delegates but instead will ask that delegates be chosen in party-run processes. This declaration pressures the states to come into compliance with the national party's rules. Where state governments have not complied, the national party then must decide what action to take. Because the national party obviously does not want to be in a position of thwarting a state, it frequently has backed down and granted exemptions—for example, in allowing Wisconsin in 1976 and 1980 to hold an "open" primary or in permitting Illinois and West Virginia to hold individual delegate selection primaries in 1980. A national party, in short, is inevitably in a negotiating rather than a simple command relationship with the states, and its ability to achieve compliance will be affected partly by which party controls the state government.

Not surprisingly, the legal questions raised by this relationship have been taken into the courts. After much confusion and conflict among lower court opinions, the Supreme Court finally has clarified the issue by denying the states any claim for forcing their delegate selection laws on the national parties. In the 1975 case of *Cousins v. Wigoda*, the Court denied the claim of the state of Illinois that the Democratic convention is obliged to seat delegates chosen in accord with valid state law. In so doing, the Court granted rather broad recognition to the national party's claim to establish its own criteria for seating delegates:

> The states themselves have no constitutionally mandated role in the great task of the selection of presidential and vice-presidential candidates. If the qualifications and eligibility of delegates to the state were left to state laws . . . each of the fifty states could establish the qualification of its delegates without regard to party policy, an obviously intolerable result. . . . Such a regime would seriously undercut or indeed destroy the effectiveness of the National Party Convention. . . . The Convention serves the pervasive national interest in the selection of candidates for national office, and this national interest is greater than any of an individual state.[12]

The state of Wisconsin's challenge of the Democratic national party rules in 1980 emphasized the same principle, arguing that the ban on open primaries was in conflict with the state's prerogative to establish the manner in which delegates were selected. The Court rejected the argument, this time definitively, contending that even if the state law placed only a minor burden on the national party, "a state or a court may not constitutionally substitute its own judgment for that of the [national] party."[13] Although the ruling does not allow the national party to require a state to enact any specific type of primary law, the party is free to deny the seating of any delegate chosen contrary to its rules.

Although the *Cousins* and the Wisconsin primary cases clearly have denied the states a constitutional remedy for stopping the Democratic national party's efforts to regulate their delegate selection processes, the decisions certainly do not prevent the states from challenging the national party in a test of political will. The national Democratic party has so far been largely—but not entirely—successful in obtaining compliance, but this may have been because most state governments in the last decade were controlled by Democrats and were unwilling to thwart their own national party. Whether either national party acting alone could hope to attain the same degree of compliance in the future is questionable, especially if the parties sought to further diminish the discretion of the states to fix their own rules. The practical limits of the national party's power to "legislate" further changes thus remain in a certain sense unknown.

The Supreme Court cases in the last decade on the issue of delegate selection, however, have clearly given the national parties a much stronger hand in relationship to the states. By recognizing the national parties as self-governing associations—a status they will hold until Congress chooses to regulate them—and by recognizing further that they are performing an important national function, the Court indirectly has built up the status of the national parties as national legislators for the delegate selection process. Barring any party rules or activities that would limit the participation of minorities, the Court has made it clear that the national parties can adopt the apportionment formulas and the delegate selection procedures that they (the national parties) deem most appropriate. This recognition of the "private" or associational status of parties has allowed, although not required, the nationalization of rulemaking that has taken place over the past decade, at least in the Democratic party. Those today who are seeking a change in the system in the direction of greater representative decisionmaking have not failed to observe that the same power that has been used up to this point to make the process more democratic could be used in the future to make it more representative.

Representation

The concept of representation includes a number of different dimensions. The one stressed thus far has dealt with the issue of the representational focus of the delegates and their resulting degree of discretion. Assemblies in which the representatives are bound to vote in a predetermined way and do not possess any independence of action are not representative bodies in the sense referred to here but are devices for recording the decisions of others. Where these decisions are made by the voters, the assembly in question constitutes a form of direct democracy, although some distortion from one person-one vote may take place because of the way the representatives are chosen. Today, for example, the electoral college is an instrument of direct democracy. Representation, by contrast, implies the capacity of members of a constituent body to use their own discretion on the decisions under their jurisdiction, acting in some degree on behalf of those who selected them.

The precise dividing line between direct democracy and representation is often blurred in practice, as representatives who are legally free to vote at their own discretion may, in practice, be virtually bound. No matter where the line between these two concepts is drawn, however, the shift in the nominating process in the recent reform period clearly has been away from representative discretion. Through a variety of changes in party rules and state laws, the representational focus of the delegates has shifted in the case of most delegates toward binding the delegates on the convention's most important function—the choice of the nominee. Convention delegates remain free to decide on the platform and the rules, and if ever there were a deadlock on the first ballot of the nomination vote, most delegates would regain their discretion. Under current arrangements, however, for reasons already explained, multiballoted conventions, although possible, do not appear to be very likely.

Before 1976, the binding of delegates to vote for a specific candidate was, strictly speaking, an action of the states or state parties. Nothing in the rules of the conventions required the delegates to abide by their pledges, and the delegates therefore could have their votes counted and recorded at the convention no matter whether they kept or broke their commitment. In 1976, however, the Republican national convention adopted a rule to enforce state-imposed delegate commitments. President Ford's supporters, fearful perhaps that some of his delegates from primary states might defect despite their pledges, managed to put through the so-called justice resolution, requiring all delegates pledged under state law to vote accordingly. In 1980, that resolution was repealed, and the matter of enforcing pledges was returned to the states.

In 1980, the Democratic convention endorsed an even stronger measure than the 1976 Republican measure enforcing delegate pledges. The controversy over this measure resulted in what many at the time called the "great debate" on the "open" convention. Although this debate touched on larger questions about the representative character of the convention, in reality the issue under consideration was a narrow one, in that the proponents of representation did not call into question any of the national party rules of state provisions that bound the delegates. The sole issue was whether delegates who were already chosen as committed delegates should be forced by a national party rule to vote at the convention as they had been mandated. The question, put more simply, was whether delegates who were already messengers would be transformed into automatons. The Democratic party measure that was adopted went further than the Republican "justice resolution," since it enforced commitments not only under state law, but under party rules as well; and it added a draconian method of enforcement, indicative of the diminished representative role of the delegates, that allowed the candidates to replace recalcitrant delegates under their pledge:

> All the delegates to the National Convention shall be bound to vote for the presidential candidate whom they were elected to support for at least the first Convention ballot, unless released in writing by the presidential candidate. Delegates who seek to violate this rule may be replaced with an alternate of the same presidential preference by the presidential candidate or that candidate's authorized representative(s) at any time up to and including the presidential balloting at the National Convention.[14]

There is a second dimension to the concept of representation that deals with the questions of who the representatives are and on whose behalf they are acting. Analysis of this dimension involves a consideration of the key variables of who has the power to choose the representatives, who influences their behavior, and how the representatives themselves understand their role. It is quite clear, however, that a discussion of these issues is only meaningful to the extent that the representatives have the freedom to act on their own discretion.

One of the great ironies of the recent period is that reformers have spent so much energy discussing these issues at the time that their most important decisions have made them almost irrelevant. When a delegate is already bound on the central issue facing the convention, the interest he represents has already been defined, and it is of no importance, except perhaps for symbolic purposes, whether the delegate is white, black, male, female, old, or young.

The reformers put themselves into this paradoxical situation by proceeding simultaneously along two lines without appreciating the conflict between them. The problem of representation in 1968, as most reformers defined it, was that the convention was too narrowly based, favoring the interests of the party organizations. The party organizations were said to be deficient on two grounds: first that they neglected or underrepresented certain groups, principally blacks, women, and young people; and second that they failed to represent adequately the views of individuals whose prime focus was on issues and who could not, therefore, be subsumed under any interest group. According to the Hughes Commission, the forerunner of the McGovern–Fraser Commission:

> ... the increasing education and affluence of the electorate generally have combined to erode substantially the role of well-defined interest groups in presidential politics. ... Whereas bargaining among representatives of party organizations once could be said to represent the interest and views of the mass constituency of the party, the decline of the interest groups behind the bosses has undercut that rationale.[15]

The McGovern–Fraser Commission's solution to the underrepresentation of these interests was on the one hand quotas, which would assure proper representation for certain underrepresented groups, and on the other hand a participatory process that removed the advantages that party organizations once enjoyed and that, at least in theory, allowed the positions of the issue-oriented individuals to be represented. The best method of representation in the second instance was thought to be the voter's expression of a candidate preference with delegates bound to the proportional shares of voters favoring each candidate.

Of the two innovations in representation—assuring groups representation and registering general opinion—the latter has clearly been dominant, and the candidate preference of the delegate has now become the focal point of the delegate selection process. Indeed, it eventually fell to the candidates and their representatives to balance their delegations among the various demographic groups. To ensure the candidates the capacity to balance properly the various groups (as well as to ensure the fidelity of their delegates), candidates were given the right to approve delegate lists. Delegates from these various demographic groups were therefore not directly representative of their groups but were representatives of the candidates. Since 1972, the Democratic party has abandoned strict quotas for all groups except women, who in 1980 were guaranteed half of the delegate slots. Affirmative action provisions, however, remain in effect. In the Republican party, steps were taken in 1972 to encourage positive actions to include minorities and women, but no formal quotas or guidelines were adopted. (The demographic composition of the delegates is shown in Table 3-4.)

As observed, the representation of these "groups," often by the device of quota or quotalike provisions, has been rendered largely meaningless by the fact that representatives are now bound in their choice. However, the change undoubtedly has some symbolic significance, and it has practical import insofar as the delegates possess discretion on questions other than the choice of the nominee. In fact, with the decision of the presidential nominee already made by the voters, there has been a tendency on the part of the specially designated groups—as well as those not so designated—to push for recognition of their group interests in the party platform, often without taking into account the implications for the candidates' chances to be elected.

Table 3-4. Blacks and Women as Percentage of National Convention Delegates.

	Democratic		Republican	
Year	Percent Black	Percent Women	Percent Black	Percent Women
1952	1.5	12.5	3	11
1964	2	13	1	18
1968	5	13	2	16
1972	15	40	4	29
1976	11	33	3	31
1980	14	49	3	29

Source: CBS News Delegate Surveys, 1968–80; and data compiled by Howard L. Reiter from numerous published sources.

While the reforms have eliminated for the time being most of the practical significance of the questions of who the delegates are and on whose behalf they are acting, it is clear that these questions cannot be ignored in the context of any discussion to return discretionary authority to the delegates. A representative decisionmaking process must be justified not simply by the fact that it can exercise discretion, but that it can exercise it well. The concept of representation implies that the representatives must act on behalf of their constituents, meaning that they must at a minimum know the basic sentiments of their constituents; equally important, however, they must be able to deviate from the express wishes of their constituents to serve their best interests. Representation, in other words, has both an expressive, democratic function and a discretionary, aristocratic function. Few theorists of representation have ever conceived that these functions would best be fulfilled in an assembly that attempts to be a demographic mirror of its constituents. In fact, insofar as an assembly may need to exercise an independent judgment, the principle qualification of the representatives should be their ability to make prudent choices, which is a capacity unrelated to demographic characteristics. It remains true, nonetheless, that an assembly's ability to take into consideration the sentiments of its constituents becomes doubtful to the extent that important groups are excluded or dramatically underrepresented.

In the past, the representatives who had the greatest decisionmaking authority at the conventions were the party leaders and elected officials. A study of Democratic delegates at the 1948 convention estimated that over one-half of the delegates had held, or held at the time, a major position in a state party. This figure remained relatively constant until 1972. Furthermore, descriptions of delegate behavior in the past indicate quite clearly the influence that these party leaders had on the decisionmaking process. In 1972, the delegates holding a major position in the state party fell to 33 percent. An even more striking decline occurred in the case of the Democratic party's elected officials. In 1968, 68 percent of the Democratic senators, 39 percent of the Democratic representatives, and 83 percent of the Democratic governors were delegates or alternates to the convention. By 1976, these figures had declined to 18 percent, 15 percent, and 47 percent, respectively.[16] This decline was so great that the 1980 rules included an "add-on" provision guaranteeing that in primary states part of the at-large delegation must be chosen from party officials or officeholders.[17] These delegates did not, however, represent the organization's interest in the sense they once did, for they had to be chosen to represent candidate preferences in the same proportion as the elected delegates. Even so, the recognition in the party rules that party officials require "affirmative" protection illustrates just how completely the reforms succeeded in their original objectives of dislodging them. No similar studies dating back as far as 1948 have been conducted for the Republican party, but studies since 1968 have shown little change in the percentages of major Republican party officeholders (senators, representatives, and governors) who have attended the conventions.[18]

The debate today on the question of representation in the nominating process has raised a series of difficult factual and normative questions. Most scholarly inquiries have sought to measure the current system's performance against its own apparent goal of representing mass opinion in the nominating decision. On this point, it is asked whether those who participate in the primaries and caucuses in part constitute a reasonably representative cross section of the party's constituency or the public; and whether the opinion reflected in the primaries and caucuses is genuine and valid, rather than a distortion produced by the idiosyncracies of the schedule of the primaries and by the effects of mass media coverage.

On the response to these questions may hinge a large part of the current debate on the nominating process, for if the current system is judged inadequate by its own standard of selecting the popular choice, then people may be more willing to accept the possibility that a representative decisionmaking process could better realize this same goal. But in the final analysis, the choice between these two systems cannot be made solely by reference to these factual questions. The ability of a system to select the popular choice, while important, is not the only value by which to judge the nominating process. Other considerations that need to be taken into account include whether an assembly should be able to make its own choice on the nominee in order to satisfy criteria of competence and confidence as judged by political elites; and whether party leaders should be given more power in selecting the nominees in order to help maintain and strengthen our political parties.

THE NOMINATING PROCESS IN OPERATION

The Sequential Arrangement of Delegate Selection Contests

During the period when the mixed system was in effect, state governments or state parties had complete autonomy in scheduling their delegate selection processes. While the primaries have always been scheduled within the calendar year of the election, some of the nonprimary states chose some or all of their delegates during the previous years. This practice, which isolated the selection of delegates from the immediate tides of any nominating campaign, was considered by the McGovern–Fraser Commission as one of the prime examples of unfairness in the selection process, and under the commission's rules, all of the Democratic party's selection processes were brought into the calendar year of the election. In 1980, the rules specified that no process was supposed to begin before March 11, but exemptions were granted in several instances. The Republican party has no national rule governing the start of the selection process, although in the last election all of its delegates, with the exception of a handful in Pennsylvania, were chosen during the 1980 calendar year.

Paradoxically, while the delegate selection process is now much shorter than it was under the mixed system, the question of its length has become an issue of much greater importance and concern under the current system. The reason is that under the mixed system the start of the active campaign was not linked directly to the start of the delegate selection process. On the contrary, the early start was one of the factors "depressing" the importance of the active campaign precisely because it chose a bloc of delegates who were not affected directly by the campaign. Nor was the sequence of the delegate selection process quite as important under the mixed system as it is today. Although early primary victories often helped a candidate to get started and gain momentum under the mixed system, the selection of the delegates in nonprimary states was, in comparison to the current system, less dependent on what happened in primary contests. The candidate preferences of the delegates were not always clearly known, and the nominating decision in any case was often made at the convention.

Under the current system, the length of the active campaign is tied to the delegate selection process because delegates are now bound to the national candidates and because, given the nature of media coverage of the campaign and of voting behavior, the outcome at any one point in the campaign vitally affects what happens thereafter. Moreover, since the nominating decision is now made during the delegate selection process rather than at the convention, the effect of earlier decisions on later ones has increased.

The sequence of delegate selection is thus of immense significance in understanding the modern nominating process. It introduces certain "biases" or tendencies, which have become a subject of intense study and analysis. The first and most obvious effect is the advantage that the current system, *relative* to other systems, gives to "outsiders," that is, those who initially have little support within the party organization and who lack much public recognition. (Under any system, of course, a person who has support from these quarters is better off, but with the sequential arrangements these advantages can be more easily overcome.) The sequential arrangement begins with tests in small states (Iowa and New Hampshire), where an outsider can concentrate an immense amount of his time—which, if he is nowhere else employed, he may have in abundance—and almost all the resources as he can muster. In fact, a candidate elsewhere preoccupied—say, in a position of demanding responsibility—may find it difficult to match this effort.

It is usual to speak of the modern presidential campaign as an effort in mass politics, but this is only partly correct. In the period before the first delegate selection contest, the candidates, and in particular the outsiders, are likely to be vying for national attention. But the first actual delegate contests have been fought thus far in the smaller states, where it is not mass politics but village politics that is at a premium. Shortly thereafter, the campaign shifts to larger states, and the candidates no longer have the time to engage in intensive village politics. The phase of the campaign after the first contests, accordingly, is governed primarily by mass politics in which candidates relate to the voters chiefly through the media. The objective of the outsider, therefore, has been to try to turn his success in village politics into a mass phenomenon.

If the outsider can do well in these early contests, that is, either win or perform surprisingly well relative to prevailing expectation, his candidacy can take off. In fact, what is most remarkable about the current selection process is that a candidate can build a national reputation *during* the nominating campaign itself by scoring an early success, as Jimmy Carter (in 1976) and George Bush (in 1980) both did in Iowa. John Anderson (in 1980) accomplished the same feat, transforming two narrow losses in Vermont and Massachusetts into "victories" that gave him national prominence and enabled him later to launch a third-party candidacy.

Second, the sequential process tends to force a narrowing of the choices. Those who do not show promise early tend to drop out, in part because they are unlikely to do any better at a later point and in part because their funds tend to dry up. (This statement refers not to the candidates in a two-person race but to the third and fourth candidates in a multicandidate race.) This effect runs counter to the spirit of proportional representation. A proportional allocation of delegates in and of itself tends to fragment delegate support among the candidates and to give delegates to those receiving only a modest share of the vote. By itself, proportional representation should make it more likely for candidates to stay in for the entire race and thus for the conventions to be brokered affairs. But if the rules stress proportionality, the dynamics stress winners or near-winners, and this has so far been the more powerful tendency.[19]

The narrowing or winnowing of candidates is sometimes counted as a benefit of the sequential arrangement, but this judgment certainly is open to question. Any nominating process, by virtue of reaching its decision, eventually will narrow the field to one, and the critical question is whether this decision is better made during the primaries, and often in the early stages of the primary, than at the convention. The early winnowing under the current process, it is sometimes charged, takes place in states that are not demographically representative of the rest of the nation. By the time the states at the end of the sequence hold their primaries, the nomination decisions may already have been made, as occurred in both parties in 1980. The result generated by the sequence of selections may therefore be unrepresentative of the wishes of the national constituency and may effectively foreclose options in an arbitrary and unreasonable way.

Finally, the sequential arrangement builds *momentum*. Winning (or doing better than expected) creates the impression of being a winner (or of coming on strong). This impression influences the decision of voters in the next primary, creating the possibility of a growing spiral to the advantage of one candidate. It is important, however, not to exaggerate the influence of momentum. In 1976, Ronald Reagan came back strongly against Gerald Ford despite having lost several early contests, and Jimmy Carter in the same year began losing primaries during the later part of the campaign to Jerry Brown and Frank Church. Momentum, accordingly, is not the absolute that some commentators sometimes imply, although it is clear that it can put an unknown candidate into the race and create pressure for the failing candidates to withdraw.

Along with all the effects of the sequence of primaries noted above, momentum can lead to the choice of a candidate who may lack broad support. In a race involving a large number of candidates, some of whom appeal to the same general constituency, it is possible for a candidate from a different constituency to win a primary with a rather small percentage of the vote and thereafter capitalize on his momentum to capture the nomination. In the New Hampshire primary in 1976, for example, at least four candidates split the liberal vote, leaving Carter the moderate and conservative vote. With the momentum he obtained from that victory, he gained a decisive advantage over the other candidates, even though it might be argued that he was less acceptable to the party than some of the liberal candidates.[20]

The Role of the Media

The change from the mixed to the plebiscitary nominating process has taken the power of the nominating decision out of the hands of party leaders and given it to the participants in the delegate selection contests, which is to say, the voters in primaries. But if the voters have this power in a formal sense, then the real "power" lies in a sense in the total process that affects the people's responses and influences their decisions. During the campaign, the candidates attempt to win public support by contacting voters and getting across to them their appeals and messages. To some extent, candidates can communicate with the public through personal contacts and through the efforts of their organizations to persuade other citizens. For the most part, however, voters see the candidates as they appear to them in the newspapers and on television.

Technically speaking, there are four "channels" of media communication of campaign-related data to the public: paid commercials; direct access programming (for example, interviews or debates); news coverage of the candidates and their campaigns; and news interpretation of the campaign and its events. The first is completely under the control of the candidate's own organization, although some have argued that the practical consequences of advertising have been to shift power in the campaign organizations from more traditional political advisers to "media consultants" drawn from the advertising world. The second, direct programming, is largely under the control of the candidate, although access to these programs is often at the discretion of people in the media, and journalists can affect the content of the communications by the questions they pose. (The Roger Mudd interview with Senator Kennedy in 1979 is a case in point; aides to Kennedy, who acknowledged his poor performance, claimed that certain questions were not supposed to have been asked at one of the interviews.) The last two channels—news coverage of the candidates and news interpretation of the campaign—are almost entirely under the control of the journalists and editors. These are the channels that bring into play the greatest potential bias by actors in the political process other than politicians and citizens, and therefore are the aspects of the communications process that are most in need of close examination.

In covering the candidates and interpreting the events of the campaign, the news media stand between the candidates and the people, selecting according to their own judgments the information that is presented. By the amount of attention they give to the candidates and by how and what they portray of the candidates' activities, they influence mass perceptions and thereby affect subsequent voting behavior. Realizing this, candidates seek to influence what is covered—staged media events and speeches filled with applause lines are only two examples—and, especially when they are unknown, to increase the amount of coverage they receive. (A frontrunner may initially shun exposure in order to minimize negative reporting.) The influence of the media is not limited, however, to what they let the public see of the candidates. They also help to interpret the events themselves, for example, who is "up," who is "down," and which primaries and caucus races are most important. These interpretations can be highly important, for while they may not change what has already happened, they too can affect perceptions and thereby influence future voting behavior.

The media, then, are undoubtedly very important actors under the current system, so much so that some commentators have come close to claiming that the "media bosses" have replaced the political bosses as the true arbiters of the nominating process. If this is so—and it may well be an exaggeration of the media's power—it is incorrect to imply, as so many do, that the media bosses compete with the party leaders for political power. Under the current selection system, wherein the nominees are decided by the public voting in the primaries, the news media inevitably play a major role. The power of the media is not something that journalists nefariously steal from the politicians; rather, it is the natural result of a system that allows public opinion—and hence the agents that influence it—to decide the nomination. Criticisms of the media therefore might be addressed more properly to the system that gives rise to the media's influence.

In the initial stages of the nominating campaign, before the first delegate contests have taken place, journalists have the most discretion in determining which candidates will receive the greatest attention and which aspects of their campaign will be emphasized. As no real events have yet taken place, the aspirants have no "claim" on the news. It therefore devolves on the media, as a logical consequence of their coverage of the news, to make an initial judgment of the "serious" contenders in a large field of candidates. Obviously, when a candidate qualifies as "serious" under this test, he will receive more attention, which itself will increase the perception of the candidate's seriousness. The "pace setters" in making these judgments are the key reporters of the national newspapers and sometimes the television networks.[21] Reading and exchanging information among themselves, journalists tend in these circumstances to arrive at momentary collective judgments—known as "pack" journalism.

Whatever the judgment of the media at this point, however, the first real test comes in the delegate selection contests themselves. These real tests, if they do not reflect previous media judgments, impose a kind of check on the media's power to decide what should be covered. The "power" relationship between the successful candidate and the journalists shifts somewhat, with the journalists now seeking access to the successful candidates. The latter can now count on a great deal of coverage, and part of their problem becomes to avoid making a slip or controversial comment that the journalists are certain to notice. If the news media at this stage lose some of their earlier power in deciding who are serious contenders, they gain what is perhaps an even greater source of potential influence: interpreting the results of the races and what they imply for the status and viability of the candidates.

Media news coverage and interpretation accentuate the effects of the sequence noted above. Studies of the past two elections show that the earlier contests were given much greater network coverage than the later ones, reenforcing the importance of the early primaries. In 1976, for example, Michael Robinson found that the New Hampshire primary received more than three times as much television news coverage as the New York primary, despite the fact that it sent less than one-tenth as many delegates to the convention.[22] Insofar as other voters are influenced by the presentation of winners and losers by the media, New Hampshire "counts" for much more than New York. Again, however, it is false to assert that such coverage represents a distortion of the campaign. From the point of view of the relative share of the delegates in the early contests, of course, the coverage is disproportionate; but from the point of view of the news value, it is not. There is simply no way of avoiding the fact that the first tests are bound to be of greater initial interest, not only to the public but also to the candidates. While it is true that the intensive news coverage of the early contests itself adds to their news interest, creating a spiral effect, it is difficult to see how this could be reversed.

In presenting the outcomes, the media tend to emphasize the idea of a race among individual candidates with winners or losers. These results are obviously of great interest to the public and constitute a valid aspect of the "story" of the primaries, but they distort the outcome as it might be interpreted in a bargaining process. For example, in the 1976 Iowa contest, Jimmy Carter generally was portrayed as the winner, even though he finished second in the caucuses to the uncommitteds. A triumphant landslide for the uncommitted slate simply did not "fit" into the horserace paradigm governing the media's reporting. By the same token, considerations of how one constituency within the party may have fared relative to another are subordinated to the interest in the contest among the candidates. These biases add to the pressures on the weaker candidate to withdraw and diminish the chances of a brokered result.

Finally, and most controversial of all, in interpreting results of these contests the news media do not automatically give momentum to the numerical winner. Rather, the "winner" or the candidate depicted as "coming on" becomes itself a matter for interpretation. Thus, in the New Hampshire primaries in 1968 and 1972, Eugene McCarthy and George McGovern generally were presented in the television media as winners (both in fact lost), while in 1976 Ronald Reagan, who came closer than either to actually winning that primary, was presented as a loser.[23] In 1980, John Anderson clearly received a favorable verdict of "coming on" after the Massachusetts and Vermont primaries, even though he lost both contests.

Exactly what gives rise to such interpretations has been a subject of dispute. Some analysts initially attributed it to a liberal bias among reporters in the national news media, which is a view that seems to fit with the results of 1968 and early 1972. Others, however, see the nature of news itself as being a more important factor, especially news as it is produced in the competitive environment among major newspapers and television networks.[24] According to this view, the news emphasizes the new and the unusual; in fact, news can be roughly defined as the deviation of an event from existing expectations—expectations often held and created by those in the media. This understanding of news is, at least up to a point, entirely legitimate, for people naturally tend to remark upon and be interested in the new and the unusual. But if this excuses the news media from criticism, it nonetheless does not change the fact that intense coverage of events in a highly dramatic fashion can give impetus to the "news" result at the expense of the "real" results.

If this understanding of news is correct, it follows that the creation of the initial expectations against which the outcomes may be judged deviations is of great importance. Here too the media play a major role, for before a primary takes place the media help to create a benchmark against which the candidates will be judged. The candidates, moreover, enter into this "game," attempting to influence the perceptions of expectations in a way that will make the real event appear more favorable to them. (Thus, a leading candidate may try to minimize the margin of his expected victory by claiming that he is running even with or even slightly behind some of his opponents in the polls.) All this is in a sense "natural" to the whole process of reporting and interpreting, but it also gives a fictitious quality to the entire process in which a "game" becomes as important as reality itself.

There may be something more to the entire process of news coverage than a natural emphasis on the unexpected. It also may be, as some have suggested, that at least certain elements of the media consciously seek out and even attempt to build up the new and unexpected. The tendency to help make news in this sense follows from pressures on reporters and news networks to make news programs interesting and dramatic. Where there is no "movement" in the development of events, there is no "story" and therefore the danger that audience ratings may decline. All things being equal, therefore, the slant given in reporting an event is toward emphasizing what promises to maintain drama and interest in the campaign.

What has been said about the media biases in interpreting results applies equally, if not more so, to the coverage of the candidates during the campaign. Here, as some studies have suggested, the media place their emphasis on the drama of events and episodes that take place *during* the campaign. Attention is given less to what the candidates plan to say and more to what the media can find that is new and unexpected. As Thomas Patterson, a well-known scholar of the media, has written:

> Increasingly, election news has come to reflect journalistic values rather than political ones. . . . The publicity advantage that accompanies the winning of an open contest, the adverse news that follows upon a candidate's inconsequential gaffe, or the emphasis on issues that have journalistic appeal can affect the candidates' chances of gaining nomination or election.[25]

The exact effect of the news media on the campaign outcome remains a matter of speculation. Students of the media have looked at the stories that appear in the newspapers and on television, analyzed their content, and described what seem to be the patterns of their coverage. How this coverage actually influences voter behavior remains unknown. Nonetheless, assuming that media news does have a substantial impact that correlates positively with what it emphasizes, the effect is to make the standards of news influential in the outcome of the nominating decision; and if what has been said about news here is correct, it follows that the media's impact is to further deinstitutionalize the nature of the nominating process. An institution consists of laws, rules, and firmly established norms that channel behavior in predictable patterns. For good or ill, the legal aspects of the current system by themselves already have moved the nominating process a step away from the more structured arrangements of the previous mixed system because public opinion, which decides the nomination through the primary election process, is less predictable in its direction and its tendency than a decisionmaking process dominated by party professionals. With its emphasis on the new and dramatic, the news as a major influence on public opinion almost certainly increases the volatility of mass reactions.

News, then, emphasizes the new as it is judged in relationship to current expectations. In so doing, it favors movement and change, although movement and change in no particular direction as measured against any substantive standard. Against the backdrop of a world of "old-style" politicians, it may be the "virgin" nonpolitician who attracts attention; but as in the world of fashion, no sooner does this model become the norm than it may be the old-style politician who is back in vogue. In this ceaseless wheel of random change, yesterday's news may help create today's expectations, making yesterday's expectations today's news.

Yet however influential the news media may be on the outcome of presidential nomination, it makes little sense from the legislators' standpoint to inveigh against them. From an institutional perspective, criticism of the news media is usually meaningless and more often futile. It is meaningless because under a democratic nominating process criticisms of the news media, if analyzed closely, are often criticisms of the institutional rules. The current rules have established a system in which public opinion as expressed through the primaries decides the outcome. Under this system, the communication system will inevitably play a central role in influencing public opinion, and any competitive and free communication system functioning in the present state of technology would probably exercise its role in a manner that differs only marginally from the way our current communication system operates. Even if one assumes, however, that there is a great deal of choice in the character of news coverage, it is unlikely that it will change very much in response to the pronouncements of public officials or public bodies—although it might, of course, be modified over time as a result of the criticisms of analysts and scholars. In general, the legislator must take the media as a given today and ask what role and influence they would have under different possible institutional arrangements. Therein lies the path to an intelligent response by the legislator to any potential "media problem."

Voting Behavior in Primaries

While political scientists have developed elaborate models for discussing voting behavior in general elections, these have almost no relevance to voting behavior in primaries. Theories of voting behavior in general elections already assume certain "constant" factors that are a product of the electoral system, such as a limited number of candidates, a single election, and the existence of different partisan affiliations by the candidates. None of these conditions, however, applies in primaries. The number of candidates varies, there is a long sequence of elections, and all the candidates competing in a primary are affiliated with the same party, making partisan identification useless as a decisionmaking criterion. About the only parallel in voting behavior that can be drawn between the two is the context in which an incumbent runs. In this instance, whether in a primary or a general election, the contest tends to be a referendum on the incumbent's performance, although there is some evidence to suggest that voters in primaries are more willing to vote against an incumbent without being as concerned as they are in the general election with the candidate they are voting for.[26]

No systematic theory about primary voting is likely to develop, at least for some time, because each campaign is so different. Primary campaigns are a sea of contingencies, and perhaps the only "law" of primary voting behavior having any general significance is that a candidate's performance in any given primary is influenced by his performance in the preceding primaries. Doing well tends to help one do better, while doing poorly tends to make one do worse.

One of the most critical issues in primary voting behavior is the question of turnout. Voter turnout in primaries is generally rather low, in the neighborhood of about one-fourth of the voting age population in primary states, or about half the number voting in the final election. These are, of course, averages that vary from election year to election year and from state to state. In 1976, the primary voting turnout was 28 percent of the voting age population in primary states (as against a 53 percent turnout in the general election), while in 1980 the primary turnout slipped to 24 percent.[27] There also has been an apparent decline in primary turnout since the 1940s, controlling for the competitiveness of the nomination race.[28]

The variations among states within each primary year are even greater. In 1976, participation in primaries ranged from a low of 11.5 percent of the voting age population in Rhode Island to 44.2 percent in Oregon. In 1980, the range was from 6.4 percent in Rhode Island to 45.6 percent in Wisconsin (see Figure 3-1). A number of factors influence the rate of turnout in a state, including the degree of competitiveness (a close race that is still undecided will stimulate

Figure 3-1. Primary Voting Turnout, 1976–80.

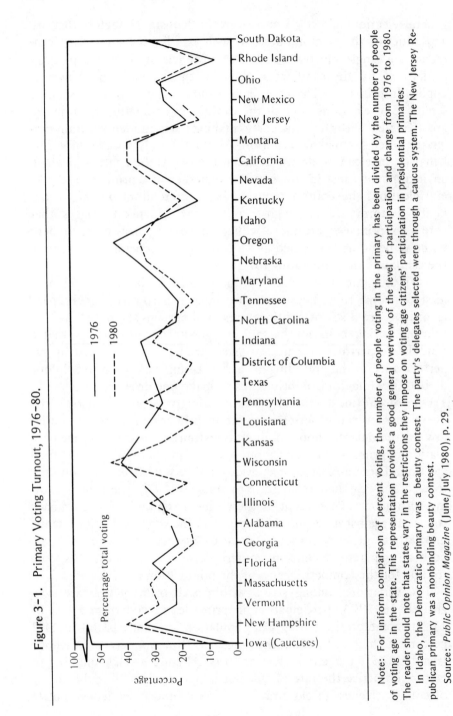

Note: For uniform comparison of percent voting, the number of people voting in the primary has been divided by the number of people of voting age in the state. This representation provides a good general overview of the level of participation and change from 1976 to 1980. The reader should note that states vary in the restrictions they impose on voting age citizens' participation in presidential primaries. In Idaho, the Democratic primary was a beauty contest. The party's delegates selected were through a caucus system. The New Jersey Republican primary was a nonbinding beauty contest.

Source: *Public Opinion Magazine* (June/July 1980), p. 29.

turnout), the amount of attention focused by the candidates and the media on a given state, the history and political culture of the state (states with a longer history of primaries tend to attract a greater turnout), and the existence of other matters being decided in the primary election (states holding primaries for other offices or presenting referenda to the voters tend to attract a higher turnout).[29]

Since primary election turnout is so low in comparison to general election turnout, there is a question about how representative the primary electorate is of the general voting electorate and the voting electorate of the party. Much research is still being done on this issue, but there is little question now that there are significant differences between the two sets of voters. The primary electorate—as Table 3-5 indicates—includes a significantly higher percentage of well-educated and wealthy voters when compared with the electorate as a whole (or with the electorate of each of the parties). These sociological differences do not necessarily mean that the primary electorates are unrepresentative ideologically of the voters in the general election, and the evidence on this point is not yet clear.[30] Most professional campaign analysts believe, however, that the primary vote, consisting of the more "activist" elements of the population, overrepresents to some extent single-interest groups and the highly ideologically minded voters at the expense of the more moderate elements of the population.

Voters in primary states must decide not only whether to vote but also, in some cases, which primary they wish to vote in. As we have seen, primary laws vary from state to state with respect to how easily voters can "cross over" and vote for candidates of the opposite party. In many states, this process is not very difficult, and the candidates compete actively for votes from independents and supporters from the other party. In 1976, for example, Jimmy Carter did well in many small town and rural areas among voters who frequently voted Republican; and in 1980, Ronald Reagan made important inroads in some states among ethnic blue-collar workers who traditionally had voted Democratic. Candidates receiving support from independents or members of the other party will often mention this fact in their campaign statements in order to persuade people of their broad appeal. Candidates who are defeated in primaries, on the other hand, sometimes will seek to minimize their loss on the ground that their opponent received votes from members of the other party, making

Table 3-5. Comparison of Democratic Primary Electorate and Democratic General Electorate, 1976 (*percentages of voters*).

State	Less Than High School Education		Black		Over Age 65		College Degree or Beyond		Income over $20,000/Year	
	Primary	General	Primary	General	Primary	General	Primary	General	Primary	General
California	11	27	12	15	9	19	34	17	35	23
Florida	13	30	8	14	23	28	28	17	26	16
Illinois	19	34	15	16	8	17	23	6	25	21
Indiana	21	40	10	11	7	24	13	6	17	11
Massachusetts	12	19	2	3	10	18	36	22	24	24
Michigan	20	30	11	22	11	17	20	10	16	17
New Hampshire	11	18	–	–	6	13	38	18	15	14
New Jersey	12	41	17	26	9	16	35	14	37	19
New York	15	31	15	20	15	14	32	19	32	16
Ohio	15	32	11	17	7	19	25	10	23	17
Oregon	19	18	n.a.	n.a.	23	13	23	20	15	23
Pennsylvania	17	32	8	15	9	15	23	15	20	9
Wisconsin	18	25	3	7	13	19	22	15	n.a.	n.a.

Note: n.a. signifies data are not available.

Source: Commission on Presidential Nomination and Party Structure, *Openness, Participation and Party Building: Reforms for a Stronger Democratic Party* (Washington, D.C.: Democratic National Committee, January 28, 1978), pp. 11–13.

the contest not truly representative of the sentiments of their own party.

On what basis do voters make their choice in primaries? Anyone who has followed the fate of candidates in the primaries is aware that tremendous swings in popular sentiment can take place during the primary season. A candidate leading by a wide margin in the polls at one moment can plummet and trail in the next. The very nature of a primary election creates this volatility. Voters are deciding among a number of candidates *within* the same party, which makes the election in effect a nonpartisan race. The tie of party loyalty, which in the general election tends to hold many voters to their party's candidate, does not apply in primaries. Although some primary contests involve relatively clear ideological choices, as in 1972 when Democratic primary participants could range as far to the right as George Wallace or as far to the left as George McGovern, in most races voters are choosing among candidates whose ideological positions do not vary greatly. Even where differences exist, the voters may not perceive them because the amount of new information they evaluate is more than they are able (or willing) to digest. From the voters' viewpoint, therefore, the candidates are often seen as essentially interchangeable. Unable to choose on ideological grounds, voters may then make up their minds on the basis of their assessment of the candidates' personal qualities or their perception of which candidates are potential winners. Both of these opinions are subject to rapid changes, as voters get to know the candidates for the first time and as the voters evaluate, with the help of the media, the performance of the candidates in the preceding contests.

Rapid shifts in voter sentiment sometimes are taken as an indication of voter ignorance or irrationality, but this conclusion seems unwarranted. While it is true that the knowledge that voters have about the candidates' positions in the primary races is often vague or incorrect, it should also be kept in mind that a great deal is being asked of the voters in this context—more, perhaps, than one can reasonably expect. One of the functions of political parties in general elections is to simplify and structure the voters' choice, allowing them to place the particular candidates within a partially familiar context provided by the history of the parties and their positions. This kind of "structuring" does not take place in primaries, and the character of the races can therefore resemble the kind of multifactional presidential race of 1824 that Martin Van Buren so deplored.

In such races, ephemeral or insignificant criteria, such as a minor tactical blunder or a media-generated wave of enthusiasm, can sometimes prove decisive.

Pollsters find it very difficult to pick the winners of primary elections in advance, and their predictions often turn out to be far off the mark. The causes of this inaccuracy lie in the many factors about primary voting behavior already discussed. Pollsters sample the entire electorate in a state, but they never can be sure just which voters will actually turn out or in which party's primary they will participate. (The more variables in a situation, the greater the inaccuracy of the polls.) Polls also, even at their best, measure voter sentiment only at the time they are taken. In a primary race, many voters are still making up their minds a week or even days in advance of the election; they may, if asked, say that they intend to vote for a certain candidate, but between the time they are polled and the time that they vote, new facts or impressions may have changed their minds. The polls in such instances are not so much inaccurate as irrelevant. They are measuring voter sentiment, but voter sentiment is highly unsettled.

Campaign Financing

Before the 1970s, financing of presidential campaigns for the nomination and final election was largely unregulated, although a number of laws enacted during this century were on the books. These laws, which included limitations on individual and group contributions and prohibitions on corporate and labor union contributions, were in many cases easily evaded and seldom actively enforced.[31]

In the past century and throughout much of this century, the final election campaigns were usually financed by funds raised by the political parties. The advent of presidential primaries and the "outside strategies" of candidates put new responsibilities on the individual candidate for raising funds, since the parties generally remained uncommitted, at least officially, in preconvention campaigns. As far back as the first full-scale preconvention campaign in 1912, candidates and commentators voiced complaints about the inequities created by the different financial resources available to the candidates. Robert La Follette, the "father" of the primary movement, accused Teddy Roosevelt in 1912 of making "lavish expenditures" and in effect selling out to "contributions from men with connections. . . ."[32]

After 1948, when the outside strategy was employed with greater frequency in preconvention campaigns, the responsibility for raising money naturally fell to the individual candidates and their personal organizations. This change in the preconvention period also affected the character of final election campaigns, for the candidates now had in place their own organizations and could assume greater control over the conduct and fundraising of the final campaign. The cost of preconvention campaigns, meanwhile, increased dramatically with greater competition in the primaries and with the advent of television advertising. Eisenhower, for example, spent an estimated $2.5 million in his 1952 preconvention campaign, an amount considered lavish for that time. By 1968, both Eugene McCarthy and Robert Kennedy spent over $9 million each, the latter in a ninety-five-day campaign.[33]

The differences in the amounts raised and spent by the candidates under the mixed system continued to be a source of comment and complaint, especially by the losing candidates. Hubert Humphrey sought to make a campaign issue of John Kennedy's well-financed campaign in 1960, and he again complained about his lack of resources in the 1972 prenomination contest against George McGovern. Losers often attempted to depict their opponents as being somehow under the influence of wealthy contributors, but these charges had only a grain of truth. Analytically, one can distinguish between fundraising capacities in two phases of the campaign: (1) prior to the campaign and up through the first one or two primaries and (2) after the initial one or two primaries. In the first phase, contributions were related to perceptions of candidate support, degree of commitment of the candidate's followers, and wealth of the candidate's supporters. In the second, while these factors continued to play a role, the more important variable was how well the candidate performed in the primaries: candidates who won or appeared to be coming on were rewarded with further contributions, while those who lost found it more difficult to raise money. Funding methods therefore tended to narrow the field in primary contests as well as to deter frivolous candidates from entering the contests.

In the 1970s, Congress passed a series of campaign finance laws, the most important of which was the Campaign Finance Law of 1974. This legislation first went into effect in the 1976 campaign, although it was suspended for a time in the midst of the preconvention campaign when the Supreme Court declared parts of the law unconstitutional in the case of *Buckley v. Valeo*. The legislation as finally rewritten to satisfy the Court's objections requires public disclosure of all contributions over $200 and limits the amounts that individuals and groups can give to a campaign. It also provides in the preconvention campaign for optional public funding on a matching basis for qualifying candidates. Once a candidate agrees to accept public funding—and all major candidates except John Connally in 1980 did so—the candidate also must accept limits on how much the campaign can spend overall and how much it can spend within each state. (For the details of this legislation, see Table 3-6.)

The campaign finance legislation of the 1970s, unlike the legislation passed earlier in this century, accomplished most of its immediate objectives, although it also spawned a number of unintended consequences that were at odds with its broader goals. The public disclosure provisions together with the establishment of the Federal Election Commission have provided workable methods for enforcing the main aspects of the legislation. Contributions from "big contributors" have been curtailed, and the direct role played by interest

Table 3-6. Campaign Finance Rules for the Preconvention Campaign.

1. Individual contributions are limited to $1,000 and contributions from political action committees (PACs) to $5,000. All contributions over $200 must be identified.

2. Candidates wishing to qualify for federal funds must raise $100,000 in individual contributions with at least $5,000 collected from twenty states made up of individual contributions of no larger than $250.

3. The federal government will match all individual contributions of $250 or less. Contributions from PACs or parties are not eligible to be matched. Public funding begins on January 1 of the election year. Each candidate (in 1980) was eligible for up to $7.3 million in public funding in the preconvention campaign.

4. Candidates receiving federal funds agree to an overall spending ceiling (in 1980) of $14.7 million plus 20 percent for fundraising; candidates also must adhere to spending ceilings for their campaigns within each state.

5. Candidates stop receiving public funds if they fail to obtain at least 10 percent of the vote in two consecutive primaries.

6. Candidates who refuse public funds are subject to the contribution limitations but may raise and spend as much money as they can.

7. Individuals and PACs may spend on behalf of or against any candidate as long as the expenditure is not coordinated with the candidates' campaign.

groups in campaign funding has been dramatically reduced. In terms of the sources from which candidates receive their prenomination campaign funds, Table 3-7 shows that the largest portion comes from individual contributors. Contributions by political action committees (PACs) have been modest, in part because funding from group contribution is not eligible for matching public funds. Most candidates have received about one-third of the total amount they raise in the nomination campaigns from public matching funds.

The other consequences of the legislation have been more difficult to determine, and the limited number of elections (two) in which the legislation has operated makes it impossible in some instances to draw definitive conclusions. Originally, many believed that the qualifying provisions for receiving public matching funds might keep some genuine contenders from receiving any public assistance. Thus far, this has not been the case, and all the serious candidates, as well as some frivolous ones like Ellen McCormick in 1976, have been able to pass the initial hurdle and obtain some matching funds. Clearly, however, the legislation has encouraged the candidates—and especially those not quite so well known—to begin their campaigns very early. Raising small amounts of funds from a large number of contributors takes a great deal of effort for any outsider. Moreover, since the first public funding installments are paid on January 2, candidates invariably will want to be in a position to collect funds at the earliest moment.

For the outsider, public funding is almost certainly a major plus and may have some incremental effect, along with the general open character of the process, in encouraging candidates to make a run for the nomination. (Indeed, some candidates may run in order to lay a claim for future nominations or to enhance their chances of being chosen as the vice-presidential nominee.) Public funding allows the outsider to add a portion of public funds to his modest amount of privately raised amounts without seriously interfering with how much the candidates can spend. As a leading scholar on current campaign funding, Herbert Alexander, has noted:

> In 1976 the matching funds helped Jimmy Carter; in 1980 the public money helped candidates such as George Bush and John Anderson, who were not well-known, and did not have ready access to significant campaign funds, to stay in the prenomination race long enough to generate sufficient enthusiasm among the electorate to mount substantial campaigns. In this way the Federal Election Campaign Act has opened up the electoral process to can-

Table 3-7. Prenomination Receipts and Expenditures of Major Democratic and Republican Contenders, 1980[a] (in millions).

Candidate	Net Receipts	Individual Contributions	PAC Contributions	Matching Funds	Net Disbursements
Democrats					
Brown	$ 2.7	$ 1.7	$ .05	$ 0.9	$ 2.7
Carter	18.4	12.9	.50	5.0	18.3
Kennedy[a]	12.1	7.2	.09	3.8	9.9
LaRouche	2.0	1.4	—	0.5	2.0
Total	$35.2	$23.2	$ .64	$10.2	$32.9
Republicans					
Anderson	$ 6.6	$ 3.9	$ .04	$ 2.7	$ 5.8
Baker	7.0	4.3	.20	2.6	7.0
Bush	16.7	10.9	.14	5.7	16.6
Connally	12.2	11.4	.28	[b]	12.2
Crane	5.1	3.5	.04	1.7	5.2
Dole	1.4	0.9	.06	0.5	1.4
Reagan	21.4	13.9	.29	7.3	18.4
Total	$70.4	$48.8	$1.05	$20.5	$66.6

a. "Draft Kennedy" movements spent $538,454 prior to the announcement of Kennedy's candidacy.

b. Not applicable.

Source: Herbert Alexander, "Financing the Campaigns and Parties, 1980" (Paper presented at Sangamon State University, Springfield, Illinois, December 3, 1980).

didates who otherwise might not have been factors in the prenomination contests.[34]

For the established candidates who could raise large amounts of money (even with the contribution limitations) and for any candidates whose campaigns take off, it is sometimes the spending limits that pose the greatest problem. These candidates may be in a position in which they could raise and spend more than the limit, but are prevented from doing so by the legislation. These limitations can lead to the paradoxical situation in which a frontrunner, having spent much of his money early in the campaign, begins to experience difficulty in mounting as large a campaign as he would like, which happened to Ronald Reagan, for example, in Texas in 1980. Among the candidates who survive the initial cut-off, the finance legislation clearly has had the effect of equalizing in some measure the amount of money that is spent. All candidates who survive the initial winnowing process are likely to face the prospect, at least in selected primaries, of being able to spend less than they could raise on their own. It is an accepted fact among practitioners in nominating parties today that the artificial scarcity of funds that prevails requires each campaign to bend every effort to make sure that money is disbursed in a "cost-effective" fashion. While this result has the (questionable) advantage of limiting the amount of money that is spent in campaigns, it also places a premium on the managerial skills of those running the campaign. Strategic errors in deciding where money is spent cannot always be corrected at a later date.

The campaign fund legislation, although important in helping outsiders get started and in equalizing expenditures among frontrunners, does not reverse the tendency of unsuccessful candidates to drop out from lack of funds. Because the public funding is based on private contributions, candidates who fare poorly still face immediate financial pressures as their campaigns lose momentum. Indeed, the gap between the failing candidates and those enjoying some success becomes even greater, as the former lose both the private contributions *and* the matching funds, while the latter gain on both counts. Campaign finance pressures, whether under the old system or the present one, have never made it easy for a candidate to reverse his fortunes and make a comeback.

There are two partial loopholes to the campaign finance legislation that need to be mentioned. The first is the formation of PACs by the *candidates* themselves prior to the time they announce their candidacies. These PACs allow the candidates to carry on their normal activities of traveling and speaking without having to count such expenditures against their spending limits. They also provide a mechanism through which national candidates can establish personal "machines" and give funds to candidates running for other offices, thus building what might euphemistically be called goodwill. The most successful such PACs before the past election were those headed by Ronald Reagan and John Connally. The use of these devices, contrary to the earlier noted effect of the campaign finance law, is to lead candidates to put off the formal declaration of their candidacies until just before public funding becomes available.

The second loophole is more serious. As in the general election campaign, individuals and PACs can spend as much money as they want on behalf of a particular candidate as long as these funds are independently disbursed and not coordinated with the candidates' official campaign organizations. The campaign finance legislation, by limiting the amount that individuals and groups (including parties) can give to campaigns, has actually served to encourage the formation of PACs and the expenditure of campaign funds outside the candidates' control. A great deal of attention was given to this problem during the general election campaign in 1980, but the potential impact of this loophole is almost certainly greater for the nomination campaign. In the general election campaign, money is probably less important as a resource than in primary campaigns because of the tremendous amount of free publicity in final election campaigns and because everyone already knows a great deal about the two major-party candidates. In primary campaigns, where free publicity is more limited and the candidates are still relatively unknown, differences in expenditures can make a greater difference, although John Connally's $12 million campaign for one delegate in 1980 should suffice to prove that presidential nominations cannot be won with money alone. Moreover, because candidates in primary campaigns are limited *in each state* in what they can spend, the infusion of an increment of "independent" funds can create significant differentials among the candidates. Thus in 1980, in the state of New Hampshire, the fund for a conservative majority spent more than $60,000 on behalf of Ronald Reagan's candidacy as his own campaign approached the state's spending limit of $294,000. This amount constituted a 20 percent increment, a figure that George Bush could not match. As Herbert Alexander has noted, "Unless the law is revised, independent expenditures will play an even greater role in future campaigns as familiarity with law becomes more widespread."[35]

4 EVALUATING THE NOMINATING PROCESS

Tom Wicker recently wrote, "Before we tinker any more with our elections system, let's take plenty of time to think through further changes before we're stuck with them."[1] Wicker's comment reflects a current widespread perception that those who have legislated change in the nominating process have taken an all too narrow approach, "tinkering" with procedural matters, such as the precise degree of fairness in allocating delegates among the candidates, while ignoring much larger issues, such as the impact of the nominating system on how candidates seek the nomination and how the nation is governed. This criticism of the reformers, whether or not it is entirely accurate, has served to focus attention on the need for legislators today to take a broader and more comprehensive approach to the question of presidential nominations. No matter what their position on the political spectrum, electoral analysts and political scientists are now asking that the nominating process be viewed in its true light as a major political institution that influences power relations and political behavior in many different areas.

Institutional theory, the name one can give to this broader approach, begins with a simple definition: An institution—or, more loosely, a regulated political process—is a structure that endures over a relatively long period of time and that, by various proscriptions and incentives, influences political behavior in patterned ways. The first element of this definition—persistence over time—distinguishes institutional aspects of the political system from temporary strategic consideration. Strategies are exercised within the context of institutions. A change in the nominating process from a system dominated by party-run caucuses to open caucuses or primaries represents an example of an institutional change: over the long run, it will produce different patterns of behavior that "fit" the new institutional arrangements. By contrast, devising a new campaign appeal—such as Jimmy Carter's plan to run as a "nonpolitician" in 1976—represents a strategy adopted to achieve an immediate objective. Usually, strategies will be limited to particular cases and change from one election to the next. Only as they persist in a general form and evolve into norms of the campaign process can they be considered part of the institution itself.[2]

The second element of the definition—influencing conduct in patterned ways—is often subject to misinterpretation. Institutions create, to a greater or lesser degree, tendencies for certain patterns of behavior; they do not guarantee a certain result. For example, although a particular nominating system may promote an institutional tendency to favor experienced and able nominees, not every individual selected under that system will possess these qualities. Other factors, such as personalities and the spirit of the times, may cancel the impact of any institutional tendency. Furthermore, certain kinds of political processes by their very nature allow for less guidance from institutions than others. It has long been known, for example, that the influence of institutional factors on the distribution of power is stronger in determining behavior in Congress than in the executive branch, since the latter is more dependent on the character of the particular person who is president. The task of nominating candidates, as we shall shortly see, is less subject to being influenced by institutional factors than most of our other major institutions.

Finally, even though an institution promotes certain patterns of behavior, it may not promote the same behavior under all circumstances. In fact, institutions can be devised so that they have the capacity under certain circumstances to promote effects different from their usual tendencies. This capacity, known as institutional flexibility, enables institutions to change their "normal" behavior, usually to meet an extraordinary challenge. For example, in the area of candidate selection, the normal tendency of the nominating conventions is to choose "moderate" leaders, but in certain instances, they may make more "extreme" choices.

Institutional theory can assist the practical deliberations of legislators by helping to identify the influences generated by an institution and by locating the particular aspects of the institution's structure that account for these tendencies. It suggests a three-step method that legislators should employ when considering major decisions affecting the basic character of an institution. First, it is necessary to identify the major aspects of the entire political system that are influenced by the institution in question. Once identified, these can be listed as the institution's potential functions. Next, the end or objective of each function must be evaluated, as must the proper balance or trade-off among them where conflicts exist. Finally, one must ask whether and how these objectives could be institutionalized, that is, put into effect by altering the elements of an institution that are under a legislator's control. (As indicated earlier, certain elements that make up the structure of an institution, such as the rules and laws and to some extent the norms, are controllable by legislators, while others, deriving from changes in social structure or technology, are not.*)

---

*As set forth in such formal terms, this approach to institutional inquiry may sound highly academic. In fact, this is not the case. The "method" outlined above boils down to the simple attempt to ascertain the contours of a problem, the objectives being sought, and the possibility that these objectives can be attained. As these steps are taken not one at a time, but in a continual process of checking and adjustment, there is nothing in this method that is impractical or that differs from the problem-solving approach now commonly used in other areas of policymaking.

Nor is the approach suggested by institutional theory deductive or given to the vice of encouraging constant meddling. The disposition to tinker might, of course, be the consequence of a theoretical approach if legislators ignored past experience in determining their objectives and blithely assumed that whatever values they happened to favor could easily be put into practice. Institutional theory, however, should serve to check this disposition. If properly employed, it demands a careful consideration of how institutions actually operate. From the discipline this study imposes, the legislator is more likely to gain an appreciation not only of what objectives are possible but also of the great complexity of institutions, the interconnectedness of their parts, and the fragility of some of their structures. Far from leading to an overestimation of what abstract reason can accomplish, this kind of study is likely to make one aware of the high probability that any change that is proposed, whether or not it ever attains the end for which it was designed, will also precipitate unforeseen consequences that may be more significant than those that were intended. So complicated is the web of forces that holds an institution in a given state of equilibrium that political science, at least in its present form, simply cannot account for all the factors at play and thus cannot assure any given outcome. Though clearly supportive of a cautionary attitude, this limited view of the capacity of political science is decidedly not a counsel for inaction. Legislators must make a judgment about the health of any institution or aspect of it, and if it is found to be unsatisfactory, they may assume the risks of attempting change, even with the near certainty of provoking unforeseen consequences.

Obviously institutional change in any political system is not always the product of systematic institutional theory. Political motives—that is, struggles for immediate advantage and power—inevitably play a role in changing institutions, especially in an area like presidential nominations, where an intense struggle for power by different interests and candidates is so close at hand. The changes motivated by these political struggles sometimes produce beneficial results and sometimes not, but from the standpoint of institutional theory, the outcome is the result of chance. Once, however, legislators begin to look at institutional change, not with an eye merely to gaining some political advantage, but with a concern for constructing a better institution, then it only makes sense to proceed by a method that promises to put reason to work to produce a beneficial result.

Despite the intense political pressures operating on legislators in this area, a striking number of legislators in the past have proceeded with the aim of institutional improvement uppermost in their minds. The present moment, free as it is from the most intense kind of political pressures, offers a rare opportunity to consider the question of presidential nominations from a detached perspective. Although relying on institutional theory will certainly not end all disagreements or guarantee perfect results, it should at least help prevent the frequent errors that result from the failure even to consider the possible implications of institutional changes.

The basic properties or functions of the nominating process can best be understood by exploring five simple questions as they relate to the process:

1. What constitutes legitimacy in the nominating process?
2. What kinds of candidates does the nominating process promote or discourage?
3. What behavior and strategies on the part of presidential aspirants does the nominating process promote or discourage?
4. What kind of choice does the nominating process promote or discourage for the final election?
5. What influences does the nominating process have on the governing process?

Implicit in these questions are the normative and practical considerations that must be weighed by the legislator. In each case, and then in all the five cases combined, the legislator must consider the objectives sought and the means of achieving them.

LEGITIMACY

Legitimacy is less a function than an essential property of any major institution. To operate effectively, even perhaps to endure, a major institution in a liberal democracy must enjoy the confidence of the people or, at the least, avoid their outright opposition. To maintain legitimacy, an institution normally must be regarded by the public as fair in its procedures and consonant with republican principles and basic democratic values. Without public support, an institution is likely to be challenged and then modified or overturned, as happened to the nominating process when the congressional caucus system came under fire in the 1820s and when the parties' control over delegate selection was attacked in 1912 and 1968. Political motivations usually provide the initial stimulus in such institutional crises, but they are more apt to have their way when the institution is already subject to popular disapproval.

Proponents of a particular nominating system often will claim that it is the *only* system that is fair and that enjoys popular support. For the legislator seeking to survey the range of potential options, these claims of legitimacy should be treated for what they usually are— "weapons" in the political struggle to establish a particular system. The legislator needs to step back from the immediate claims and examine the general principle on which the legitimacy of a system *could* be based. Even though a particular principle of legitimacy might be able to win the support of the public more easily than another, which is clearly a point in its favor, *any* principle that could pass the test of legitimacy deserves consideration; and if a given principle permits the adoption of a system that promises superior performance on other grounds, its claim to legitimacy needs to be defended. On institutional matters, even more than on policy matters, legislators bear a responsibility to help create a basis for legitimacy by explaining and defending the rationale for the principle they adopt.

But what, in particular, can confer legitimacy on an institution? In our system, there are three possible sources of support: the Constitution, representative decisionmaking, and direct democracy. The Constitution, which provides one basis of support for our major national institutions, including the "undemocratic" Supreme Court, is inapplicable in the case of the nominating process because our nominating institutions developed outside the strict regulation of the Constitution.

Without the Constitution to confer legitimacy on the nominating process—a fact, incidentally, that may account for its instability over the course of American history—proponents of different nominating systems have had to justify their claim to legitimacy by reference either to direct democracy or to representative decisionmaking (or to some combination of the two). The Founding Fathers' original constitutional plan was based entirely on the representative principle, not only for the "nominating" phase, but also for the election. Their defense of representation was twofold: first, that it could serve on certain occasions as a filter to screen out popular aspirants who were unqualified or mere demagogues; second, that it could serve most of the time, *even better than a direct popular election*, to select a person who enjoyed the broadest support of the people. These two defenses, although obviously in conflict on any one given decision, are not contradictory as components of an institutional system. Both can be performed—that is, the representatives can know the popular choice but then choose to ignore it in order to check a possible mistake in the people's judgment.

The Founders' preference for a representative body to perform the democratic function of selecting the preferred popular choice was based on the fact that in the case of any open, multicandidate contest—and remember that the Founders envisaged a form of nonpartisan politics—there is usually a scattering of votes among a number of candidates, none of whom may have the initial support of anything approaching a simple majority. A representative decisionmaking process, in this instance, can be the best device to overcome the problem of fragmentation and select the popular choice. This problem of fragmentation is intrinsic to any popular electoral system that is normally faced with more than two major alternatives, a point that has frequently been made by modern political scientists when discussing the idea of a national presidential primary:

> A primary, like a referendum, is a device for registering and counting already-formed first preferences. It has no way of identifying, let alone aggregating, second and third choices so as to discover the candidate with the broadest— as opposed to the most intense—support. And since broad support is much better than narrow but intense support for unifying the party [nation] and appealing to the general electorate, this is a serious deficiency.[3]

The development of party competition, which took place in two stages between 1796 and 1836, ended at least one of the justifications for representation at the final election stage. Since the party system now narrowed the choice to two individuals—at least most of the time—the public could make the democratic decision itself by popular vote without any need for help by representatives. As for the other justification—filtration—this function also was assumed by the political parties.

During the period in the 1820s when party formation was taking place, there was a great deal of opposition to the concept of party nominations. President Jackson, initially one such opponent, proposed in his first annual address to Congress a new nonpartisan selection process, consisting of a direct national popular election with a run-off between the top two candidates, provided no one received a majority in the first round. Jackson sought thereby to take the "winnowing" function out of the hands of private associations (parties) and give it directly to the people.[4]

Proponents of political parties rejected this plan, seeking instead to have party nominations recognized—albeit unofficially from a legal standpoint—as the normal means of narrowing the field. The nonpartisan ideal, they argued, ignored the fact that people naturally seek to form associations in order to promote certain ends or purposes beyond those represented by the personal ambitions or programs of any one individual. Parties were associations of such a nature, frequently encompassing very broad and diverse coalitions, but coalitions that still had some general purpose. Democracy, party proponents argued, was better served by allowing such self-governing associations to form and compete than by fostering a system of competition among individuals who advanced their own record or personal popularity. Martin Van Buren, the major defender of political parties, argued this point when attacking the nonpartisan system that had temporarily developed in 1824:

> In the place of the two great parties arrayed against each other in a fair and open contest for the establishment of principles in the administration of government, [there were] personal factions having few higher motives for the selection of their candidates or stronger incentives to action than individual preferences or antipathies. . . .[5]

Competition between parties, in Van Buren's view, constituted the proper kind of democratic system in contrast to a specious democratic system based on competition among "independents," each building anew his own constituency every fourth year.

In transferring the winnowing process from a nonpartisan mechanism to parties, something more than a mere substitution of functions occurred. While the parties did assume the representative functions of narrowing and filtration, they also added the new idea that competition for the presidency was not simply a competition among individuals but was in some measure a competition between political parties. It is precisely this notion that Americans have at times resisted, preferring to view the presidential selection process in a nonpartisan light and resenting the "special status" of the parties. The public's ambivalence about parties, at least during certain periods, has meant that attacks on party prerogatives have often met with a sympathetic response, and the party system has frequently been in danger of being undermined by appeals to Americans' antipartisan sentiments.[6]

The existence of parties did not entirely suppress the problems of candidate recruitment and democratic legitimacy. It merely moved them back one step. The parties had themselves to find a way to select a candidate who could command the support of the broad base of the party membership (the "democratic" function) and who could best promote the interests of the party and serve it—and the nation—if chosen president (the "filtration" function). To perform these functions, party defenders from Martin Van Buren and Thomas Ritchie in the 1820s to Austin Ranney today have asserted the need for a representative decisionmaking process that accords a good deal of weight to party leaders. For example, in 1824, Thomas Ritchie noted:

> The elements of this great community are multifarious and conflicting and require to be skillfully combined, to be made harmonious and powerful. Their action, to be salutary, must be the result of enlightened deliberation.

And in 1978, Austin Ranney said:

> A strong presidential party, in my view, would be led by a mix of national and state party leaders—governors, state chairs, state legislative leaders, U.S. senators and representatives, national chairs, Presidents and ex-Presidents— whose influence with the national convention's delegates was so strong that when a coalition of leaders agreed on who the candidate should be, the delegates would follow their lead and choose him.[7]

The modern case against representative decisionmaking is based precisely on an unwillingness to give party leaders—and perhaps even parties themselves—the discretion to choose the nominees. The foundation for this modern view was first established during the Progressive era. Whether the Progressives merely opposed the existing form of political parties or whether they were opposed to parties altogether was a matter that had little practical significance at the time. In either case, given their animus against the corruption and localistic character of existing parties, the Progressives sought to undermine the existing political parties by the easiest and most readily available means—an appeal to direct democracy in the form of presidential primary. For the Progressive party, the existing parties were "tools of corrupt interest . . . knowing no allegiance and accepting no responsibility to the people."[8] For Robert La Follette, the cure was to "go back to the first principles of democracy, back to the people."[9]

It is worth observing that in these calls for direct democracy, the Progressives made no mention of the need to perform any of the functions of representation that formerly had been carried out by the conventions. If the Progressives' rhetoric is taken at face value, their argument was not simply that the parties had been performing the functions poorly, but that no institution had the right to perform them at all. The criterion of democratic legitimacy excluded any kind of choice other than that made directly by the people.

During the turmoil that preceded the Democratic convention of 1968, many people again raised the democratic standard of the Progressives. The New Politics advocates attacked American parties on the identical grounds of their Progressive forebears, calling for a reform that would allow the people to speak directly through direct national primaries. The reformers within the party councils, while sympathetic to many of the complaints of the New Politics advocates, did not share their hostility to parties as such. They did, however, begin by conceding that the battle over the principle of legitimacy in presidential nominations was over. The first of the reform commissions, the Hughes Commission, reviewed the course of events since the Progressive era in the following terms:

> The fact that many states declined to provide delegate selection entirely by primary was acceptable to the nation—but only because the system did not override or frustrate the national commitment to direct democracy in the naming of presidential nominees. . . . [By 1968] a confluence of forces has

made the Democratic National Convention an occasion of great moment in the inexorable movement of Presidential politics in America toward direct democracy.[10]

The McGovern–Fraser Commission began more or less from the same point, using the fact that the issue of legitimacy was settled to prove how moderate its proposals were and the necessity of accepting them. The party system, its official report argued, was faced with the genuine threat of a change to a national primary. In order to stop this change, which the commission felt would totally destroy parties, reforms were needed. The commission implied that it was doing the most that could be done for parties under the circumstances. As two recent defenders of the reforms argued:

> . . . those who condemn the party reforms as too radical must at least concede that they headed off worse possibilities. Public opinion polls throughout the late 1960s and 1970s showed whopping majorities of Americans cynical about political parties, politicians, and institutions, and strongly in favor of a national primary, abolition of the electoral college, and establishing a binding national initiative.[11]

Clearly, reforms in the selection process were needed in the late 1960s. Public confidence in the existing system, as the reform commissions argued, had eroded, and the pressure for other alternatives was real. Yet whether or not the reforms had to move the system so dramatically in the direction of direct democracy is far from certain. The fact that the reformers did *not* intend to increase the number of primaries seems to indicate that the pressures for change left substantial room for the exercise of discretion. Perhaps the alternative of reforming the representative decisionmaking process, rather than undermining and virtually abandoning it, was not adequately explored at the time. In any case, the climate of the 1980s is very different from that of the late 1960s. The assault on representative institutions in the 1960s was a generalized phenomenon, directed not only at parties but at the entire political system. The selection process, it appears, bore the major brunt of that assault, although it was not the only institution to undergo democratic reforms in the last decade. Now that that spirit of democratic reform has subsided, legislators may wish once again to consider whether or not they "gave in" too quickly to a temporary public mood.

The history of our nominating process indicates a tradition of support for two basic principles of legitimacy: first, for representative decisionmaking, understood as a process whereby parties retain discretionary judgment in deciding the nominees; and second, for direct democracy, understood as a process whereby the people decide the nominees, whether through a nonpartisan direct election, through direct national primaries, or through a system similar to what we have today. The main arguments on behalf of each principle are easily summarized.

Defenders of representative decisionmaking contend that it:

1. Protects and promotes political parties, which ultimately offer the public the best means of exercising a democratic choice.
2. Allows the parties to determine which candidate has the broadest support.
3. Provides a "filter" that on rare occasions can screen out certain candidates whose popularity may be great, but whose nomination might be detrimental to the party and the nation.

Defenders of direct democracy respond that it:

1. Promotes mass participation in the choice of the nominees—a desirable goal.
2. Avoids putting the decision in the hands of some group that inevitably will reflect an interest other than that of the public at large.
3. Represents the only system that the American people today are willing to accept.

Assessment of Legitimacy Under the Present System

Legitimacy, as noted earlier, refers to the perception on the part of the public of an institution's fairness and adherence to republican principles and democratic values. That perception presumably is influenced in the long run by relevant arguments and evidence, especially the sort of evidence that, when brought to the public's attention, might well change its perceptions. Accordingly, in discussing the question of legitimacy, one must consider not only the public's *current* perception of legitimacy but these other issues as well.

Discussions of public preferences on institutional matters rely frequently on poll data. Some of the defenders of reforms, for example, cite evidence in the polls indicating that direct democracy is now the accepted principle of the American people. Yet, as most careful students of public opinion would concede, the polls on such questions of institutional preference may indicate little more than dissatisfaction with the current performance of an institution. If public opinion is understood as a settled opinion based on a real consideration of the alternatives, it is doubtful whether polls on most institutional issues represent public opinion; they actually may represent the public's answer to a particular question on a particular day—in effect, an opinion created by the poll itself. Only a persistent reading of a dominant preference, backed by other evidence that that preference would stand up in the course of execution, constitutes the expression of a valid public opinion.

In the 1950s and 1960s, polls taken on the question of the nominating process consistently revealed opposition to the existing system. Five Gallup polls taken between 1952 and 1968 showed that a majority of the American people—and in three polls over two-thirds—favored adopting a national primary over the existing convention system. After the reforms, a majority still favored a national primary over the convention system, with only a slight decrease in the percentages. Indeed, by 1980, more than two-thirds of the American people again indicated their preference for a national primary.[12]

How should such data be interpreted? On the one hand, it could mean that the public genuinely favors a national primary and finds even the current system undemocratic. On the other hand, it might indicate merely that the public has been dissatisfied with the performance of the last two nominating systems. In fact, before taking too seriously such evidence of dissatisfaction, the possibility should be considered that any conceivable nominating system, because of the controversial task it performs, might be unable to win broad public support in opinion polls.[13]

It might well be, as some now maintain, that the public wants—and has come to expect—a direct say at some point in the nominating decision. Yet if this is the case, it is clearly impossible on the basis of current poll data to determine at exactly what point the public would become more dissatisfied with marginal movements toward greater representative decisionmaking in the nominating process. The polls, accordingly, cannot be of much help in predicting the potential level of support for many of the proposals currently under consideration. Nor, of course, can they predict the effect on public opinion of a new consensus on the nominating system among political leaders.

Turning now from perceptions of the legitimacy of the current system to arguments and facts, two basic perspectives on the issue of direct democracy in presidential nominations can be identified. The first claims that mass participation in the nominating process is not, after all, very important; the second states that, to the extent it may be important, the present system is far from being perfectly democratic; indeed, it is severely flawed in many important respects.

The first of these perspectives is clearly the more "radical," contradicting what now appears to be an accepted consensus. Nevertheless, the position might serve as a corrective to any further movements toward direct democracy and a partial justification for a movement in the opposite direction. The essence of this position is stated in the simple declaration by the late E. E. Schattschneider, a noted political scientist: "Democracy is not to be found *in* the parties but *between* the parties." [14] In this view, the entire direction of the recent reforms, which is based on the idea that intraparty democracy is essential, is mistaken. A regime can be democratic without mass participation within the nominating process so long as the public is presented a reasonable choice at the final election. In fact, in every other modern democracy, with the possible exception of France, the candidates for chief executive are chosen by either the party organizations or the party members in the parliament. [15]

A problem frequently raised, however, is that limiting the choice of nominees to a representative process within the two major parties forecloses the expression of a valid democratic choice because the major parties themselves may not adequately represent the wishes of the American public. This problem, however, may not be as serious as many suppose. For most of its history, presidential recruitment in the United States has been by two major parties, and groups dissatisfied with the major parties have possessed the legal right to begin a third party. This right has been exercised frequently enough for the leading scholar of political parties of the last generation, V. O. Key, to explicitly characterize the American electoral process as a two-and-one-half-party system. [16] The option to form third parties which will be discussed later in more depth, considerably strengthens the case for the legitimacy of a party-governed representative nominating system. An electoral process open to third parties provides a fair chance for any excluded group, even if one concedes that the major parties enjoy considerable advantages by virtue of their established organizations and the loyalty of their followers.

The other perspective on legitimacy under the current nominating process begins by questioning the extent to which the current system actually meets its goal of being truly democratic in the sense of accurately representing the wishes of the rank and file of the public. To be sure, the number of citizens now participating in the nominating process has risen dramatically since the reforms, partly because of the increased participation rates in caucus states but mostly because there are now many more primaries. The primaries, even with their rather low turnout rates, involve on the average a much higher number of participants than caucus proceedings, although a few caucus states actually have had a higher percentage of participants than some primaries.[17] Even with these higher participation rates, the electorate that votes in the primaries is, as we have seen, far from being demographically representative of party voters in the general election. Moreover, not all the citizens who participate in primaries have a meaningful voice in the selection process, for by the time many of them have the chance to vote the outcome may have been all but decided. Thus, in the 1980 contests, by the time the final primary day arrived, giving nearly one-fifth of the potential voters their chance to vote, the results of both parties' races were already a foregone conclusion. Finally, if the news media play anything like the major role that many claim for them, there is room for questioning whether the public is exercising power in the manner depicted by advocates of direct democracy.

Defenders of the current system will no doubt point out that these problems of representation are likely to be even greater in the case of current caucus procedures, where the level of motivation required to participate is much higher than that for primaries and where, as a consequence, there is an even greater probability of the results not truly reflecting the wishes of the rank and file or the public. Yet the question of whether the results are skewed is a function not simply of how many people participate but of who the participants are and the nature of the role of the representative. Distortions occur in a process in which most of the participants are advocates of particular candidates or causes and where these participants are motivated to turn out at rates that differ dramatically from their proportion in the party and the electorate. Where the participants and the delegates instead view their role as general trustees rather than agents, the problem of distortion can be minimized; and paradoxically—although quite logically—a representative result may be more likely in the nominating process where participation is low and where the participants or the delegates view themselves as having a proprietary obligation to represent the interests of their party.

It is clear, however, that caucuses can produce great distortions, as in 1972, when well-organized antiwar groups flooded some of the Democratic mass meetings and won an unexpectedly large share of the delegates. But there are other methods besides selection by caucuses to promote a deliberative process. One method currently being considered by the Hunt Commission of the Democratic party is to allow some of the delegates to be chosen ex officio, that is, by virtue of their positions and without regard to their candidate commitments. If these delegates include elected officials from the party, such as governors and members of Congress, the parties will be assured of having a pragmatic group of delegates that has met the test of standing for election and that is free of the distorting effects created by differential participation rates during the selection process.

THE QUALITY OF THE CANDIDATES

Every legislator is presumably in search of a nominating system that will produce "great" presidents on a regular basis. This search, however, is somewhat like the quest for the Holy Grail—obligatory, perhaps, but unlikely to reach its goal. In the first place, "great" statesmen are not always in ready supply. Greatness, alas, is a rare quality— the analogue of true genius in the arts. Second, there is no system that the human mind can devise that can guarantee the discovery of political greatness, even when it exists. The qualities that make for greatness in leadership are not, like those that constitute athletic prowess, easily seen or judged. In Adam Smith's words, the skills of the potential statesman are "invisible . . . always disputable and generally disputed."[18] There is, accordingly, no science for the selection of leaders. All might agree on the importance of such attributes as experience, maturity, prudence, and the ability to inspire, but of these only the first is (partially) measurable. Ultimately, the qualities of leadership must be determined according to human judgment by a group more or less qualified to make that judgment.

A nominating system, as it influences the type of character who is elevated, consists of certain legal criteria and norms of leadership, the group designated to choose, and the process by which that group makes its decision. These constitute the institutional components of the nominating process. They combine to produce certain tendencies as to the type(s) of persons nominated—but *only* tendencies. Because in any system there is room for judgment, the choice made under a given system can never be fully predicted. The more discretion granted to a system to go outside certain specified channels, the greater the range of choice that may result, perhaps risking error for the chance of discovering talent. (Keeping to normal channels, however, also can produce dramatic mistakes.) The fact that a given system produces a bad prime minister or a bad president is no proof, therefore, that that system is faulty, and legislators must resist simplistic analyses that use mistakes as the sole grounds for changing the system. Because all leadership selection systems are based on the fallible judgments of human beings, they are all partially lotteries; but this is no argument for making them into total lotteries.

Comparing the British system of nominating candidates for prime minister with our presidential nominating process illustrates the influence of different selection systems on the kind of individuals who are selected. In the British case, the leadership model is rather specific: the person chosen is invariably a member of Parliament who usually has had a record of experience in national affairs through service in past governments. The candidates are judged by a rather limited group—the parliamentary party—that knows the candidates directly and has had the chance to judge their political skills through close observation. According to many defenders of the British system, this combination of factors tends to produce qualified and experienced leaders and lends a general stability and predictability to their entire leadership selection process.

The American nominating system, by contrast, has for quite some time been more open than the British system, in the sense of choosing individuals from different offices and backgrounds. Because of the constitutional doctrine of separation of powers and because the conventions formerly were comprised mainly of delegates with strong ties to the state parties, being a member of Congress was no advantage in securing the nomination. Governors were often in a much better position, and even today, when the national media give an edge to highly publicized senators, the last two presidents held the gubernatorial post as their last elected office. Lateral entry from fields outside politics has also been possible. Under the mixed system, for example, the Republicans in 1940 nominated a businessman who had not held elective office (Wendell Willkie) and in 1952 selected a famous military hero (Dwight Eisenhower). Some observers have been critical of the American system for promoting candidates who lack sufficient experience in national politics, but many have defended it for precisely this openness and capacity to broaden the search beyond the scope of those holding national elective offices:

> A presidential system of government in which future chief executives need serve no apprenticeship in comparable office is a risky venture. But a system of leadership selection requiring a long period of training and testing in a prescribed set of offices has problems, too—the dangers of stagnation, of inflexibility in changing times and circumstances, and of development of a self-perpetuating elite.[19]

Comparing the British and the American systems sheds light on the general way in which a nominating process can affect the type of candidate who is elevated. Because the differences in this case are so clearly tied to the basic nature of the two systems of government, however, an examination of the comparative results among different systems under the American experience may be more useful.

The Founding Fathers expected to elevate individuals with established records of service; they envisioned no popular campaign as such, but rather a conferring of the office on someone who had *already* distinguished himself and acquired a broad national reputation. The congressional caucus system did not change this tendency, although it added to it the prerequisite of partisan leadership. The congressional caucus system, in actuality, was if anything more disposed to insiders, as it was the congressmen and not locally selected electors who were charged with narrowing the field of potential candidates. The caucus system has quite properly been compared with the British system of prime ministerial selection; and it has been argued that if the caucus system had continued, the U.S. government might well have evolved along British lines, with the president being "responsible" to his party in Congress.[20]

The shift to the convention system had the effect of opening the selection process to individuals outside the narrow cadre of leaders in Congress or the administration. The convention was a broad-based institution with roots in the states and localities. Moreover, when the final election process became more democratic after 1828, the parties had to find candidates that had a strong public appeal. As the parties at this time were also broad and heterogeneous bodies, it was necessary to select nominees who could hold together the various elements of a diverse coalition. The general tendency of this system was to elevate "politicians" able to perform a brokering function, or else—on occasion—military heroes who could unite the party (because they had no connection with earlier political infighting) and give it a special edge in the contest for votes in the final election. The reliance of parties in several instances on military heroes indicated that, while parties controlled the mechanism of nomination, the American people retained a desire for nonpartisan leaders.

Both types of candidates favored by the convention system suggest a rather cautious or moderate kind of leader not given to upsetting the status quo. Perhaps this was a problem, as many frequently complained of the absence of dynamic leaders. Yet it is a testimony to the flexibility of the convention system—and perhaps an indication of the nature of parties themselves—that on occasion the conventions chose staunch partisans known for their ability to articulate a political viewpoint, for example, Lincoln, Bryan, and Wilson.

The Progressive idea of candidate selection—and it only slightly affected the actual practice of nominating politics until the recent reforms—was quite different. According to the Progressives, the most important quality of the nominees was the capacity to galvanize the public during a campaign through a high-minded kind of popular leadership. In contrast to the Founders' system or the congressional caucus system, a candidate's previous record was not as important as the candidate's performance *during* the campaign. In addition, unlike the convention system or, for that matter, the mixed system, the Progressive ideal put little value on brokering or coalitional leadership. Rather, it envisioned a dynamic leadership that would stake out new and bold visions, lifting public opinion and educating the nation.

Evaluation of the Quality of Candidates Under the Current System

The current nominating system has realized the basic form of the Progressives' ideal, although some would say that the results represent an intensification and even a distortion of their goals. Clearly, the most distinctive characteristic of the current system, viewed in comparative and historical perspective, is that the nominating process itself has become the principal testing ground for establishing one's claim to the nomination. Previously, of course, strategy was important, but aspirants generally did not win or lose the nomination on the basis of how they performed in the time just prior to the decisionmaking event itself. Under the current system, by contrast, performance in the campaign has become a much more important factor in determining the result. This change is not merely a by-product of attempting to make the system more democratic; it also reflects the way the selection process itself is now viewed and the greater significance attached to it. Thus, many who comment on the nominating process today believe as a matter of course that the most important criterion of any nominating system is how well it gauges the qualities of the aspirants *during* the period of the nominating campaign.

When the effects of sequence in the primaries and the influence of the media are taken into consideration, the nominating campaign often becomes not simply a test among established national contenders, but an occasion for outsiders to make their reputation during the campaign itself. In this respect, the current system is more open than the pure convention system and the mixed nominating system. Yet while it is more open to aspirants willing and able to undertake a long, public campaign, it is decidedly more closed to candidates who for one reason or another cannot engage in such campaigns. Thus, the convention system in 1916 could turn to a candidate like Charles Evans Hughes, who was a sitting Supreme Court Justice. Today, this kind of flexibility is impossible. In fact, given the amount of time it takes to campaign under the current system, it may well be that the present system gives an advantage to those *not* currently holding an official position that requires a great deal of time and responsibility. The campaigns of Jimmy Carter, Ronald Reagan, George Bush, and John Connally made some wonder whether, in Senator Howard Baker's words, it was "better to be unemployed to run for President."[21]

According to defenders of the present system, current campaigns have produced "a partial simulation of the presidency [that provides Americans with] much necessary data with which to measure politicians, as well as time to make an assessment."[22] Others, however, would argue that while the campaign does test one quality—leadership of public opinion—it ignores or downplays others. As one critic, Malcolm Jewell, has argued, "our selection procedures place a higher premium on the ability to campaign than the ability to govern."[23]

Furthermore, while most qualities that relate to a candidate's ability to govern are in some way put on display during the campaign, it does not follow that the most important ones have the greatest influence on the result. A British correspondent notes:

> A candidate's record is of less consequence than his packaging. The supreme political activity is campaigning. Anything that gets in the way of that is a handicap; hence, except for the incumbent it is a disadvantage for any candidate to hold an office that requires him to do anything more substantial than engage in perpetual electioneering.[24]

Finally, although it may sound a bit harsh to ardent democrats, some critics are now willing to state that the public alone may not be the best judge of qualities relating to the ability to govern. In the initial stage of nominating, they see the need for expert or professional judgment, what Austin Ranney has called "peer review":

> The absence of peer review means that the candidates are chosen by people who know them only as fakes on television and as personalities described by the news media; they are not chosen by people who know them personally and who have worked with them in situations of stress that show a person's true leadership qualities. Candidates are strangers chosen by strangers, not peers reviewed by peers.[25]

CONTROLLING CANDIDATE BEHAVIOR

The nominating process has a direct and decisive influence on the behavior of presidential aspirants, not only during the campaign itself but well before it. The ambition of politicians to become president constitutes one of the most powerful sources of energy and dynamism in our political system, and it is only natural that ambitious individuals will tend to mold their actions to promote their chances of becoming president. The nominating process, therefore, plays an important role in determining the kind of behavior, within a given range, that aspirants are likely to pursue in their quest for the presidency. Legislators of the nominating process must accordingly seek a system that best channels the ambition of presidential aspirants, deflecting it from behavior harmful to the political system and harnessing it, if possible, in behalf of activity that contributes to the public good.

Two examples in which different nominating systems have influenced the channeling of presidential ambition will serve to illustrate this institutional property. First, under the congressional caucus system, cabinet members who were seeking presidential nominations threatened the unity of the executive branch by courting favor with members of Congress. The nominating system was one factor during that period that contributed to a weak presidency. Second, under the current system, where building a popular constituency is the way to launch a campaign, senators seeking the presidential nomination often attempt to "use" their committee hearings as platforms for promoting their aspirations. After the experiences of 1972 and 1976, Norman Ornstein, a noted scholar of congressional behavior, wrote:

> As the Senate has opened up its proceedings . . . it has become more attractive to potential presidential contenders. . . . Many more Senators consider themselves presidential possibilities . . . and tailor their behavior accordingly, . . . increasing their legislative activity and public visibility, and emphasizing media coverage over legislative craftsmanship.[26]

Until the Progressive era, controlling and channeling ambition were among the principal concerns of legislators of the nominating process. The Founders planned their system to encourage those seeking the presidency to strive for the kind of record that would win them a reputation of distinguished service. Van Buren and some of the other politicians who favored party nominations in the 1820s had more modest hopes about the benefits that the nominating system could bring in this respect, but they agreed that one of the main reasons for establishing party competition was to avoid the dangers of individual candidate factions. In Van Buren's view, the unregulated competition of individuals for the presidency under a nonpartisan system would stir up unnecessary divisions, as each candidate would look for and attempt to keep alive issues that would maintain their popular constituencies. As Thomas Ritchie, Van Buren's close collaborator and editor of *The Virginia Enquirer*, wrote: "Ambitious struggles for power, with the bitter uncontrollable passions which they inevitably engender, are the most formidable evils which threaten free governments."[27] Where demagogic appeals were not used, there was always the danger of mere personality politics in which elections would be decided on—to use the modern terminology—images alone. Those who founded parties clearly hoped to put the party principles "above" the individual candidates, thus "compelling" them to submit to the general principles of the major parties. Ambition was channeled to make moderate leaders.

If putting party principle above the individual was the objective of the proponents of the convention system, then reversing that formula was the goal of the Progressives. To a large extent, the Progressives viewed the adherence of candidates to the outmoded philosophies of the parties as one of the main causes of national stagnation. Therefore, they sought to remove many of the shackles on individual ambition in presidential nominations, in order to give it free play, hoping at the same time to strengthen the president's claim to popular backing. The Progressives' intention was not, obviously, to create the factional politics that those who founded the convention system feared, but rather to stimulate broad and statesmanlike appeals by skilled popular leaders. The Progressives expressed their complete confidence in the principle of direct democracy.

Evaluation of Candidate Behavior Under the Current System

The current selection process makes virtually no effort to restrain or channel the ambition of presidential aspirants. Campaigns begin very early, in some instances almost two years in advance of the election; the field of candidates includes some who, but for the success of previous outsiders, seem oddly out of place running for the nation's highest office; and the system virtually demands that the aspirants openly "admit" their ambition, coyness now being rewarded with neglect.

How these effects are evaluated, of course, is another matter. The fact that candidates must confess their ambition early on may only mean an end to the hypocrisy that once was characteristic of so many campaigns. Yet this hypocrisy was not without certain incidental benefits, such as promoting a sense of dignity for the candidates and reducing the number of public campaign promises they were obliged to make. The need for an open display of ambition, on the other hand, may have the negative effect of discouraging some highly qualified politicians from devoting themselves to the single-minded effort that running for president now requires. Ambition is surely a "normal" and a desirable quality for most politicians, but it may be unwise to have it so openly encouraged. As one political scientist, Everett Ladd, has argued:

> There is more than popular confusion and tedium to the price paid for a campaign whose climactic stretch runs from the Iowa caucuses in January to

the conventions of July and August. Such a test of endurance has a devastating effect on candidate recruitment. Few people want to campaign steadily for two years prior to the convention, and few potential presidents are so unoccupied that they can drop everything for two years in order to run.[28]

The length of the current campaign has received more negative commentary in recent years than almost any aspect of the entire system. Tedium, the physical burden placed on candidates, and the near obsession that many develop for the campaign "story" have all been cited as undesirable effects of the campaign's marathon proportions. The length of the campaign and the fact that the nomination decision is made so far in advance seem to have the political and mass psychological effect of reducing by the time of the conventions the sense of freshness and enthusiasm for the candidates. Candidates who have already campaigned for over a year may appear—especially to journalists—as "old hat," and all sense of "mystery" about the elevation of leaders may be lost.

In the final analysis, the evaluation of how the current system structures ambition will probably stand or fall on an assessment of the consequences of modern popular leadership during the campaigns. Does the unrestricted right of so many aspirants to compete for popular constituencies create the risk of increased factionalism, demagogic politics, and image campaigns? And if so, are these risks worth running when balanced against the benefits of broad public education and access to new ideas and candidates of previously undetected merit?

THE AMOUNT OF CHOICE AND CHANGE

The presidential selection process as a whole should provide the public with a reasonable choice in the final election and allow for fundamental political change when the people favor it. To some extent, the entire electoral process can, therefore, be viewed as an institution that helps regulate the pace of change in society. It is essential, however, to understand the limits as well as the possibilities of institutional arrangements of the selection process in this area. Not all political change in our society—contrary to what many have implied—is generated in and through presidential election campaigns. Much of it comes from the institutions operating in response to other objectives and incentives. And to the extent that presidential campaigns can generate change, the cause certainly lies more in the nature of the times than in the nominating institutions. Periods of crisis and conflict may generate "exciting" campaigns and pressure for change regardless of the institutional arrangements, while periods of normalcy may result in "mushy" campaigns in which both candidates make vague appeals to the center. To a large extent, tensions in society and pressures for change arise independent of the electoral institutions. What the electoral institutions can do, however, is establish different tendencies toward change, seeking either to stimulate or moderate it. As these institutional tendencies interact with the "nature of the times," they can have significant effects.

The modern reform movement arose initially from the complaint that the electoral process was suppressing and ignoring the real divisions in the populace on the Vietnam War and indeed on the fundamental nature and direction of our political system. Advocates of the New Politics argued that the true objective of the nominating process could not be expressed in the time-worn phrase of political scientists that we had to "maintain strong parties." Rather, these critics demanded—and quite properly—that the party system had to be justified in terms of whether it promoted certain necessary public functions. By this criterion, the New Politics advocates found our entire "private" nominating system wanting. The two-party system, with its alleged virtual monopoly on the choice the nation was given, failed to offer the nation a much needed chance for change. This theme ran throughout the McGovern–Fraser Commission report, but it was best stated in a recent defense of the reform movement coauthored by one of the former research directors of that commission, Ken Bode:

> If there can be said to have been a single, dominant theory behind the party reform movement of the last decade, it would be this: In a country in which two—and only two—political parties can elect a president, it is important that the nomination processes in both parties afford the possibility of a genuine test of the leadership and stewardship of candidates, even of an incumbent president. If such a test is precluded at the nominating stage, then the general election choice may be hollow for many participants.[29]

What in fact were the effects of the nominating systems before the reforms in respect to the values of choice and change? For the Founding Fathers, who never envisioned partisan conflict, the answer was expressed in terms of changes of administrations in a nonpartisan environment. In general, their system was designed when the public was deeply dissatisfied with the record of an incumbent. Those who established the convention system in the 1820s were wary of an electoral system that offered too many options and that too easily translated momentary tides of public opinion into national electoral politics. Like the Founders, therefore, they sought to stabilize the initiatives deriving from the electoral process, but by a very different means. The solution they proposed was the norm of two-party competition between moderate, coalitional parties. These parties normally would control the access of individuals to the presidency, and their moderate principles along with the pragmatic interests of professional politicians would erect impediments to the intrusion of temporary movements and extreme leaders into national politics.

This system, however, while attempting to foster moderation relative to an "open" nonpartisan electoral process, was not entirely closed to new ideas or movements. There were two avenues that often worked in conjunction with each other by which new movements might force their way into the political system. The first was through the permeability of the major parties. Although usually controlled by established and pragmatic politicians, the major parties were sufficiently open to be taken over at certain times by "amateurs" dedicated to a new cause. In 1896, the Populists in the Democratic party were able to push aside the moderates and nominate William Jennings Bryan, while in 1964 the "amateur" conservative movement gained control of the Republican convention and nominated Barry Goldwater. The second avenue of access for new movements was through third or minor parties. Although new parties faced substantial difficulties in competing with the established parties, they still managed to force important policy changes on the major parties, sometimes because the major parties moved to pick up the support of a new constituency and sometimes because they sought to avoid the threat of being supplanted by a new party. The electoral process, accordingly, has never been correctly characterized as a simple two-party system. The challenge of new parties, whether actual or potential, frequently has been an important factor in American politics, and the general function of achieving the appropriate degree of choice and change in the electoral process must be judged, therefore, not by looking at the major parties alone but at the entire electoral system.

The disposition of the convention and mixed nominating systems toward choice and change cannot be expressed in a simple formula.

These systems did not encourage change but permitted it when powerful and persistent forces in the nation called for new and different approaches. This "bias" toward moderation, if this is what it should be called, was based on the premise that an openness to change risked an openness to radical movements. Furthermore, because major change is not something that the nation needs at every election, but only infrequently, institutional processes should not encourage it as part of "normal" politics. In short, the electoral process as a whole was deemed flexible enough to meet the need for choice and change even when the major parties were closed as judged by current standards.

Evaluation of Choice and Change Under the Current System

Proponents of direct democracy, from Progressives to the New Politics advocates, never accepted this bias in favor of moderation. They have been committed to just the opposite: where defenders of the convention and mixed systems have spoken of imposing restraints on new movements, proponents of direct democracy have spoken of stimulating them. Their bias has been toward progress and new ideas. As James Sundquist has written:

> The reforms of the twentieth century have gone a long way toward ensuring that whenever the country polarizes on an issue, the polarization will be quickly and faithfully reflected by the parties. . . . This prospect will encourage more politicians to take their chances with extremism, giving it even greater potential. This is the hazard of an open party system.[30]

The modern reform movement was predicated on the assumption that the major parties alone bore the responsibility for promoting change and that third-party activity was ineffectual and suspect. The great battles over policy and direction, in this view, must take place within the major parties, and the major parties, therefore, have a quasi-public obligation to represent fairly all elements within the electorate. (This notion seems to conflict, however, with the Democratic party's goal of limiting primary and caucus participants to party members.)

The reformers' case against the efficacy of minor parties rested on two dissimilar concerns. First, in 1968, minor parties faced tremendous legal hurdles in securing access to the ballot in many states.

These hurdles consisted of inordinately high petition requirements—
in some instances over 10 percent of a state's voters—and early filing
deadlines. Ironically, these hurdles were an indirect consequence of
the reforms of the late nineteenth century, which, to prevent corruption and fraud in voting, gave to the states the power not simply for
the administrative purpose of running effective elections but also for
the promotion of the "public" function of protecting two-party
competition. The norm of two-party competition that Van Buren
favored was converted into a *legal* doctrine, as states attempted to
limit minor party access to the ballots. Since 1968, however, this
situation has changed dramatically through intervention by the federal courts. George Wallace successfully challenged an Ohio law that
protected two-party competition, and in 1980, John Anderson managed to lower further the legal barriers to entrance of minor parties
or independent candidates.

Today, the influence of the legal system on third parties is, therefore, very different than it was in 1968. Minor parties, including
those like John Anderson's that form at the very last moment, enjoy
much greater access to the electoral process. Minor parties perhaps
suffer a slight disadvantage in fundraising in comparison to their situation before the last decade, in that they must now raise funds under
stringent campaign contributions laws without receiving any public
assistance. If, however, a minor party obtains over 5 percent of the
nationwide vote, as John Anderson's independent campaign did in
1980, it receives a pro-rata share of public funding after the election
and automatically is given the same share in the next election. The
curious effect of this legal intervention in the regulation of parties
may be to provide artificial support for certain minor parties after
they have served their immediate purpose of registering discontent.

The reformers' second point of attack on the efficacy of minor
parties rests on the observation that they have not managed to win
the presidency, or even threaten seriously to do so, since the formation of the Republican party before the Civil War. Dismissing third
parties on this ground, however, may well be a case of confusing
cause with effect. Third parties may have been "incapable" of mounting a serious threat, not because it has been impossible for them to
do so but rather because the major parties have managed to remain
responsive to the major currents of American politics. Indeed, the
development or threat of development of minor parties has helped
to force the major parties to remain responsive to public issues.

Under this understanding of the electoral system, therefore, the success of the major parties in maintaining their duopoly has been the result of their own efforts. Had both these parties become rigid or unresponsive, they could have been—or could still be—replaced, even as the new Social Democratic party in Great Britain now threatens to replace the Labour party. To be sure, third parties begin at a disadvantage because of their organizational resources and the absence of an existing pool of partisan adherents, but these need not be insuperable obstacles. In fact, conditions today make it much easier in both of these respects for third parties because organization in an age of the mass media counts for less than it did in the past and because there are many more self-described independents in the electorate.

The reformers' insistence, therefore, that the burden of handling the function of choice and change rests exclusively with the major parties is an exaggeration. To the extent that it constituted a valid claim in 1968, because of existing legal barriers, it is much less so today after the Court decisions of the past decade; and further changes in the law could easily remove any unfair disadvantages for minor parties. In short, an open and democratic electoral process— that is. a process open to third parties—can serve as an alternative to direct democracy within the parties as a means of promoting the broad objective of maintaining a capacity for choice and change in the electoral system.

There seems to be little question, however, that the reform movement has opened the major political parties and thereby the political system as a whole to a *more* rapid penetration of new movements. At a minimum, the primary path to the nomination has provided greater access to candidates who seek to redefine what the parties stand for, and in recent nomination contests, many aspirants have run on programs that allegedly have been designed to build fundamentally new coalitions. Although such attempts may have reflected in part the condition of electoral instability caused by the decline of the once solid New Deal coalition, they probably also follow from the very nature of the new system. To justify their quest for the office, candidates frequently must present themselves as offering a new formula for American politics that will bring together previously unconnected elements of the populace. Offering oneself merely as the traditional standard-bearer for the party may not be sufficient. This incentive to attempt to form new coalitions can, of course, be destabilizing, eroding the very stability of a party that enables it to *sustain* change over the course of several elections. The result could be a greater appearance of change with less capacity in the political system to effectuate it.

Yet the experience since the reforms were initiated is sufficient to demonstrate that these "new" movements need not always be issue-directed or ideological. In 1976, Jimmy Carter won the nomination by blurring many of the issues and by emphasizing broad themes like efficiency and honesty in government. The success of his appeal not only surprised ideological liberals within the Democratic party but also caused them to reconsider whether "openness" in the nominating process actually does support more choice and change. The limited number of cases to analyze makes generalization very hazardous, but the logic of the system seems clear: The new system is indeed more open to new movements or moods, which, depending on the nature of the times, may or may not be ideological; in some years, therefore, there may be more ideological choice than the previous system tended to promote, but in other years, perhaps, much less.

Finally, the quality of "moderation" associated with the previous nominating systems was a result not only of a representative decisionmaking process but also of the particular characteristics of American party organizations since the 1830s. Although by no means devoid of ideological commitment, the organizations were often dominated by persons concerned with victory and with maintaining jobs and patronage for the local party. This incentive gave the leaders of these organizations a certain pragmatic cast of mind, known in the literature of political science by the term "professionalism." Yet party organizations need not be led by professionals in this sense. In many other countries, the most ideological individuals are often the ones who join the parties and dominate their internal organizations. In Britain, for example, the current leaders of the local organizations of the Labour party are decidedly more left of center than either the members of the party in Parliament or their voters; and as they struggle to gain more influence in the leadership selection process, they show every indication of attempting to force their ideology on the British people.

Much the same concern has been voiced about the possible character of American parties in the future. Indeed, as we have seen, there are some today who favor the primaries, not because they stimulate more choice and change, but rather because they moderate the kind of choice in comparison with what it would be if modern party organizations select the nominees in a representative decisionmaking process. In this view, modern party organizations in America, like some of their counterparts in Europe, are likely to be dominated by ideological amateurs, and the people are needed to "save" the parties from their own organization leaders.

Accordingly, legislators today must be certain not just to establish certain institutional forms based on past performance but to ask what goals or ends those forms will promote under present circumstances. Judgments of a practical sort must be made. While the evidence today clearly suggests that American parties will never again be dominated by the kind of professionals who dominated them in past years, there is no reason yet to think that future representative processes must inevitably be dominated by ideological amateurs. Contrary to the situation in some European systems, there is less of a tradition of ideological politics in America; and the large number of electoral offices at the state and local levels almost certainly will ensure a more pragmatic point of view among the ranks of the party members. If they are ever given the responsibility for making the nominating decisions, so-called amateurs might quickly begin to behave more like professionals.

INFLUENCE ON THE GOVERNING PROCESS

The emphasis that the reformers placed on the functions of legitimacy, choice, and change led them to ignore a connection that past legislators considered fundamental—the influence of the nominating system on the character of presidential leadership and on the relationship between the presidency and the Congress. The nominating system does not, of course, have as direct or as profound an influence on these matters as the constitutional provisions and laws that set forth the basic outlines of presidential and congressional power; but the nominating system can have a significant effect on these institutions, complementing or undoing institutional tendencies that have been established to govern their operation. One of the legislators' goals, accordingly, should be to devise a nominating system that promotes—or at any rate does not detract from—these objectives.

For the Founding Fathers, this goal took precedence over all the others. They viewed the selection process as the means and governing as the end. Each aspect of the selection process was designed to complement a governmental objective. To ensure the president's independence from Congress, the Founding Fathers provided the executive with a base of electoral support apart from the legislature; to maintain the president's partial distance from the immediate pressure of public opinion as well as to remove the possibility of an extraordinary claim for enhanced extraconstitutional power, they devised an indirect electoral scheme of selection by special representatives; and to keep the president above factions or preexisting electoral cleavages, they sought to prevent the formation of political parties and establish a nonpartisan electoral system. As events turned out, some of these planned influences of the selection process proved to be the least durable of all the institutional tendencies that the Founders tried to establish, but they serve nonetheless to illustrate a method by which legislators can approach institutional reform in this area.

For those who established the doctrine of party competition in the 1820s and the 1830s, the influence of the nominating system on the governing process was perhaps not as important a question as was regulating the pace of choice and change and controlling candidate ambition. Yet these legislators were still concerned with such problems in the governing process as the decline of party competition along with nomination by the congressional caucus, which threatened the president's base of electoral independence. The combination of renewed party competition and nomination by convention removed that threat. These legislators were also looking for a mechanism that could provide a connective link between the president and Congress at the level of policymaking without undermining the essential constitutional prerogatives of either institution. The political party could perform this function by serving as an extraconstitutional instrument for assembling authority in a system in which separation of powers made coordination a difficult problem. Indeed, not only did parties provide a link between the president and Congress, but they also linked both to an organizational network that operated throughout the nation. This network provided a potential source of support for national leaders, even while it sometimes limited their discretion. Curiously, it was Woodrow Wilson who best articulated this contribution of the parties:

> [Power] can be solidified and drawn to the system only by the external authority of party, an organization outside the government and independent of it, . . . a body that has no constitutional cleavages and is free to tip itself into legislative and executive functions alike by its systematic control of the personnel of all branches of the government.[31]

Despite this praise for parties, Wilson, along with the Progressives, sought to destroy the parties, at least in their existing form, in order to raise the presidency to a new and higher plane in the American political system. Whatever the benefits of the parties, the Progressives believed that they extracted far too high a price in terms of corruption, localism, and weak presidential candidates. Like the Founding Fathers, Wilson and many of the Progressives saw clearly the relationship between the selection system and the governing process, although they appeared to go much further than the Founders in thinking that the presidency could be *changed* in large measure through the influence of the selection process. In the Progressives' view, a stronger presidency would emerge—and one less tied to pluralistic interests—by eliminating the traditional party and allowing presidential aspirants to appeal directly to the people. The president's new base of support would be public opinion, a force that would either allow a president to "compel" congressional acquiescence without a party (the nonpartisan Progressive vision) or else enable the president to control his party (the partisan Progressive vision). Under this system, presidential leadership would be the force that would replace parties and combine the various power centers in a separation-of-powers system.

Modern reformers, who began their call for institutional change at the very moment when doubts were surfacing about an imperial presidency, were obviously in no position to assert that the nominating process should be used to strengthen the president's power. Indeed, as observed, the reform movement offered little systematic analysis of their proposed changes on the governing process. The effects were implicit. At least for the early New Politics adherents of 1968, the overriding purpose of the selection system as it influenced the governing process was to empower leadership that would be responsive to public opinion, which at the time was conceived of as on the verge of being radical and change-oriented. The electoral system, in other words, was designed to promote populistic leadership, a tendency foreshadowed by the Progressives but advocated with less restraint by modern democratic enthusiasts.

Evaluation of the Influence of the Governing Process

The function of the nominating system's influence on the governing process was "rediscovered" by political scientists during the administration of President Carter. Because of this recent rediscovery and the limited time frame in which analysis was conducted, political scientists faced the problem of disentangling the influences of the nominating system from other influences that operated during the same period. Some, unfortunately, may have overinterpreted the effects of reform, attributing virtually every failure of the Carter administration to the institutional decline of parties and ignoring personality and ideological factors, such as President Carter's clearly "non-political" approach to governing and the lack of consensus in the Democratic party. To avoid this error here, it is only necessary to recall that this discussion refers to institutional tendencies and, in the case of the effects of the nominating process, to second-order or indirect consequences.

The absence of a representative decisionmaking process has weakened one source of the president's support from other political leaders, including members of Congress. Because these leaders have no direct say in choosing their nominee, they are less likely to feel a bond of commitment or the need to cooperate. They are in no sense accountable for the choice of the nominee, as they had no voice in his selection. Yet it is precisely the support from these leaders that a president needs to govern effectively. Public opinion is no substitute for this support. Quite the contrary, public opinion as a resource of extraconstitutional presidential authority has often proven to be a weak and fickle reed on which to rest political power. As Richard Rose, a well-known political scientist, has written:

> To become a party standard-bearer, an American politician must first of all *divide* his party by contesting primaries against fellow partisans. . . . Presidential candidates may spend years in building a political following, but it is first and foremost a *personal* following. . . . Rootless candidates risk becoming rootless in government. Insofar as a politician concentrates his attention upon the relatively contentless concerns of campaigning, distancing himself from any organization besides his own personal following, he loses a stable commitment of party loyalty to invoke against the sub-governments of Washington.[32]

The current method of pursuing presidential nominations encourages a form of campaigning and leadership that emphasizes divisions, since it is often only by dividing that candidates can activate a popular following and differentiate themselves from their opponents. In comparison to previous selection systems, the current system creates more incentives to promote the differences among factions and fewer incentives to weld these factions together into broad and relatively harmonious coalitions. If the great challenge of governing in American politics requires a curbing of the "mischiefs of faction," then the new system has made the president's task only that much more difficult. Coalitions today, when they form, are created in spite of, and not because of, the current nominating system.

The long and exposed presidential campaign also tends to encourage a kind of popular leadership that promises too much to too many groups and that relies on slogans to excite popular constituencies. These practices may have something to do with the rise of expectations that have been engendered by presidential campaigns, a rise that is perhaps inevitable where so much weight is placed on courting popular favor. Paradoxically, the need to court public favor, especially on a state-by-state basis, may lead to even greater pluralistic pressures and concessions to various interest groups. According to one political scientist, Jeffrey Fischel, the number of specific promises that candidates make over the course of the campaign has increased dramatically over the past two decades.[33] These special appeals are often made in a particular speech or a specialized advertisement, whereas the general appeals made in higher visibility communication media tend to be more image-conscious or ideological. The very problems of demagogic leadership and purely image appeals that Van Buren identified in 1824 may now be endemic to the modern selection process and may in turn have created problematic models of political leadership that influence the public's conception of the presidency.

Finally, there is the effect of the length of the campaign on the governing process. While an election campaign is in progress, and while the public begins to focus its attention on the prospect of a change in power, "normal" politics is put into a state of suspension. Power is partially drained of its steady constitutional basis, as everyone begins to think of the possibility of a new administration with new programs. The nominating process does not, of course, change the date of the election itself, but by intruding the active campaign for the presidency much earlier into the final year of a president's term, it changes the climate in which a president must attempt to govern.[34] For an incumbent seeking renomination, the problem is even greater. The same adverse side effects of "incumbent politics" in presidential campaigns that were identified by Alexis de Tocqueville long ago are now pushed back earlier into the term of each president who is challenged for his party's nomination:

> [During the campaign] the President, for his part, is absorbed in the task of defending himself. He no longer rules in the interest of the state, but in that of his own reelection; he prostrates himself before the majority, and often, instead of resisting their passions as duty requires, he hastens to anticipate their caprices.[35]

The length of the current process also poses a serious problem in the case of a president who is popular within his own party, but who, for personal reasons, might wish to retire after one term. To respect the "spirit" of the process as it now exists, the president would be obliged to declare his intention not to run at least nine months before his term expires, in order to allow candidates to engage in primaries and caucuses. Such a step, however, might not be in the interest either of the president or the presidency, for the president would forfeit an important source of his authority—the belief on the part of others that he might be in office for the next term. This problem is one that has never been discussed, perhaps because the chance of its occurring seems so unlikely. Yet it represents more than a hypothetical possibility, and it would leave a president with the uncomfortable choice either of sacrificing needlessly part of his authority or engaging deliberately in an act of dissimulation by insisting, up to the time just before the convention, that he intended to run again.

Many have defended the reforms in the nominating process on the grounds of their greater fairness and openness, but few who have studied their effects on the governing process have rendered a favorable verdict. Whatever modest gains the new system may have brought us in legitimacy, they do not seem to have been worth the price that has been paid in effective governing.

5 OPTIONS FOR CHANGE

Institutions, like works of architecture, are complex structures. They cannot be judged one part at a time with each part measured against an abstract standard of perfection. They must be looked at as functioning units and judged by the criteria of the best fit of all objectives within the same structure. Responsible criticism of any institution, therefore, cannot stop at merely pointing out apparent deficiencies; it should propose other plans that promise to achieve better results than the existing structure. All thought about institutional change should be based on a consideration of the merits of alternative plans, all of which are bound to be defective in some respects. The question in the final analysis is not whether the existing nominating system has failed, but whether there is an alternative that can work better.

Those considering institutional change also must ask whether the benefits that might result from reform outweigh the risks and costs of tearing down or modifying existing structures. Generally speaking, there are two basic orientations toward political change held by groups known as "reformers" and "conservatives." Reformers are disposed to jump in and make changes whenever a plan seems to offer a chance of making some improvement. Confident of the legislators' power to control human institutions, reformers generally consider the risks of undertaking change to be minimal. Only, perhaps, when reformers are defending their own handiwork from attack do they act out of character and resist innovation. Even then, however, their natural instincts will sometimes prevail, as evidenced, for example, by the tenor of Senator Lowell Weicker's comments in recent testimony on the status of the current nominating process:

> I am not prepared to support the status quo. . . . I am usually one of the last to condemn reform, and it is even a bit awkward and contradictory in the present instance, because we are here to discuss further reform, and I am for it.[1]

Conservatives are generally more averse to risk when it comes as institutional change, believing with Edmund Burke that "to innovate is not to reform" and also holding that many of the effects of any change cannot be anticipated in advance. As political scientist Edward Banfield has written:

> The changes that we intend when making a reform, if they occur at all, are always accompanied by others we do not intend. These others may occur at points in the system far removed from the one where the change was initiated and be apparently unrelated to it. Commonly changes produced indirectly and unintentionally turn out to be much more important than the ones that were sought.[2]

Caution is clearly the watchword here, and those who agree with Banfield will probably accept the spirit of Viscount Falkland's dictum that if it is not necessary to change, it is necessary not to change. Even this statement, however, concedes that change is sometimes needed, and many conservatives believe that this point has been reached and surpassed in the case of the nominations process. More important, the conservatives' usual reluctance to test the icy waters of reform does not apply in this instance because the existing rules for the nominating process are not the tested "gifts" of years of prescription and tradition, but instead the recent creations of their reform-minded peers. In fact, most of the changes are so recent that they have only begun to produce unforeseen consequences, more of which will become visible to us as time goes on.

Today, then, may be one of those unusual moments when both reformers and conservatives may be prepared to join together in a serious consideration of alternatives to the current nominating process. The range of options they will be willing to entertain, however, will depend on what they both can agree is within the realm of possibility. Many reformers of the last decade proceeded on the publicly stated assumption that the American people would be unwilling to accept a nominating system based on anything other than direct democracy. If the reformers continue to hold this position, or if legislators accept the trends of the last decade as somehow irreversible, then the basic choice is limited either to rationalizing the current system or to implementing a system that is even more democratic. Instituting a system based on a greater degree of representative decisionmaking would be impossible. If this old position of reformers is rejected—and there is much evidence among its spokesmen, old and new, to suggest that it has been—then the full range of practical options can be opened to debate.

OPTIONS FOR CHANGE: A CLASSIFICATION SCHEMA

Legislators of the nominating process can change the system by moving in one of three different directions: (1) instituting more direct democracy; (2) altering the status quo to rationalize it; and (3) establishing a system having a much greater degree of representative decisionmaking by the political parties. The first two options are in one sense variations on the same theme, since the status quo is already based essentially on direct democracy. Nevertheless, as there is still some room on the democratic flank of the current system, the alternative of further democratization must be considered.

It is not sufficient, however, merely to analyze the intended direction of change. Another issue for the legislator to consider is the level of authority to use for initiating the change. There are today three basic sources for legislating on the nominating process: (1) the federal government (by ordinary laws or by constitutional amendment); (2) the national parties; and (3) the states and state parties. This issue of the source of change is of great significance, not only because it has a direct bearing on questions of feasibility, such as whether a particular level of authority is likely to act, but also because certain consequences flow from the use of each level of authority regardless of the direction of change that is being sought. For example, using the federal government to legislate change, no matter what the plan, will change the legal status of American national parties and further incorporate them into the legal framework of the political system.

These two dimensions—direction of change and source of legislative initiative—provide the basis for classifying the plans for changing the nominating process. They are presented below in Table 5-1, and the discussion that follows in this chapter will take up first the attributes of each source of authority and then the specific plans grouped by the direction of change. If this twofold classification schema is more complicated than past scholarly treatments of alternatives, it is because the entire matter of legislating change has become more complex. Fifteen years ago, before the reforms, there was a near perfect correspondence between the basic kind of nominating process people favored and the source or level of authority then advocated to control the rules of the nominating process. Nearly all those calling for more direct democracy envisioned action by the federal government in the form of national primary legislation, while those wishing to maintain or improve the representative system wanted authority left with the states and state parties. Today this correspondence no longer holds. Not only is there now an additional level of authority for legislating change (the national parties), but there are also differences in which direction change is being pursued on each level. Thus, as Table 5-1 indicates, legislation by Congress has been suggested to promote all three basic objectives: more democracy, rationalizing of the status quo, and greater representative decisionmaking. This complexity requires the more elaborate treatment outlined above.

A final word must be added about the use of the term "plan" to describe the various proposals for change. An institutional plan in the strict sense refers to a coordinated set of steps designed to change the existing institutional arrangements in a concrete and specific way. The intended outcome can be articulated and its merits weighed against other plans. But institutional change need not always take place in this way. Another method of change is to alter the constraints under which certain authorities operate, allowing them to make changes according to their own interests and assessment of the situation. As distinct from change by means of a plan, this method initiates a *process* of institutional transformation. The central legislator may make some calculations about what these authorities are likely to do, but the proposal, strictly speaking, is limited to altering the power relations among existing authorities. The outcome is left undetermined. "Process" changes of this sort will be included in the alternatives considered below.

Table 5-1. A Classification Schema for Plans to Change the Nominating Process.

Directions of Change	Sources of Change		
	Federal Legislation	National Parties	States and State Parties
More democracy	Direct national primary plan Mandatory regional primary plan	Adoption of further "democratic" reforms[a]	Adoption of more primary laws[a]
Rationalizing the status quo	Restricted primary date plan Optional regional primary plan	Restrictions on the length of delegate selection process	Creation of voluntary regional primary groupings[a]
More representative decisionmaking	National primary (Ladd proposal)	Adoption of steps promoting representation or removal of requirements against ex officio delegates and for proportional representation	Elimination of primaries Use of authority returned from national parties to institute steps promoting representation

a. Plans not discussed in this chapter.

THE SOURCES OF LEGISLATING CHANGE

The Federal Government

From the first bill for a national primary brought before Congress in 1911 through the most recent such proposal made in 1980 by Senator Weicker, more than 275 pieces of legislation have been introduced that deal in one way or another with "nationalizing" the nominating process—bringing it under the direct control of federal law.[3]

These legislative proposals range from a direct national primary with a run-off, to mandatory regional primaries, to federal regulation of the dates for state primaries. If the number of such proposals alone can be taken as an indication of interest in such legislation, then the pressure for change has been growing. Since the era of reform began in 1968, 121 of those 275 bills have been introduced, and there is no indication that the activity on behalf of such initiatives will cease. As Austin Ranney recently remarked, "Proposals for some kind of federalized presidential primaries are now being discussed more widely and seriously than for decades . . . [and] such discussion is likely to increase rather than diminish."[4]

Of course, these numbers can be read in two ways. Of the almost 300 proposals made, Congress has taken floor action on only three occasions (1947, 1950, and 1952), and in none of these instances did the legislation come close to obtaining a majority in either House. The absence of support for such legislation may indicate a strong consensus against federalizing the nominating process. Yet the history of nationalization on other issues counsels against making confident predictions. Expansion of federal authority traditionally has faced strong initial opposition. For whatever reason, however, an idea will suddenly take hold, and soon everyone is debating not whether something should be done but how it should be done.

An important question in the effort to nationalize the nominating process is whether it can be carried out by means of ordinary legislation rather than by constitutional amendment. Nearly all the proponents of nationalization assume that the nominating process falls within the legislative powers of Congress, for the bills introduced to change the process have been in the form of regular legislation. Yet enough doubt remains on this issue that some legislators would probably oppose any such legislation on constitutional grounds and challenge it in the courts. These objections would in all likelihood grow stronger as the legislation in question moves from simple regulation of state primaries to outright federal control of the entire nominating process—a move that would strip the political parties of their traditional role in making the nomination decisions.

The case against the constitutionality of legislation in this area is based on the simple, if nowadays naive, claim that the Constitution does not give any such power to Congress, either directly or by any obvious implication. The sole provisions relating to presidential elections refer to the selection of *electors*: Congress has the power to determine the time of their choice and the date on which they vote.[5] It is true, of course, that the Founding Fathers originally intended this stage of the process to be both the nominating and electing stage and that the "escape" of the nominating process from constitutional jurisdiction was something they never envisioned. Yet excluding the Twelfth Amendment, nothing was ever added to the Constitution to respond to the development of party nominations. Indeed, when the whole question of party nominations and the presidential selection process was raised during debates in Congress in the 1820s, the proponents of political parties made it clear that they were offering the device of party nominations as a "private" settlement of the problem and as an alternative to pending proposals for constitutional amendments.[6]

Congressional elections under the Constitution are treated very differently than presidential elections. Again, nothing is said about the nominating process, which was not foreseen, but Congress is given broad powers in Article I, Section 4, to pass laws regulating "the times, places and manner of holding elections for senators and representatives." It can preempt state laws in these areas wherever it chooses. Relying on this broad language and on the precedent of state laws connecting primary elections with general elections, the Supreme Court in the case of *United States v. Classic* (1941) held that federal power in congressional contests applied to primary elections no less than to general elections.[7] Although Congress has not exercised its power over primaries nearly as much as in general elections, its full legal authority over primaries seems beyond dispute.

There may, of course, be a certain logic to assuming that Congress should have the same control over presidential elections as it has over congressional elections. Justice Hugo Black certainly seemed to think so in his opinion for the Court in *Oregon v. Mitchell* (1970), a case dealing with the constitutionality of federal law lowering the voting age in elections for federal office to eighteen years (the decision has since, in effect, been superseded by the Twenty-fifth Amendment). "It cannot be seriously contended," Black wrote, "that Congress has less power over the conduct of presidential elections than it has over congressional elections."[8] Such a statement, now the conventional wisdom, makes it easy to ignore the small inconvenience of the Constitution's different wording in the two cases.

Yet if there is a logic to assuming that Congress does have the same control over the two electoral processes, there is also a logic to assuming that it should not. The convention debates and the *Federalist Papers* clearly show that many of the Founding Fathers were concerned with protecting executive independence from legislative interference. Making the president's method of selection substantially independent of congressional control was a means to this end. The very limited discretionary control that the Constitution gives Congress over presidential elections therefore probably reflects a concern over the basic question of separation of powers. Even though the nominating process was never mentioned in the Constitution, the same general principle would still apply.

Legal precedent has by now established that Congress has the power to regulate aspects of presidential elections and primaries on such matters as campaign contribution limitations and public financing. But this power—based on the Supreme Court's view in *Burroughs v. United States* (1934) that Congress has the implied authority to "preserve the departments and institutions of the general government from impairment or destruction, whether threatened by force or by corruption"—is very different from a plenary power to assume outright control over the entire process.[9] Although the weight of precedent and scholarly opinion now inclines toward the view that Congress does possess the power to act in this area as it sees fit, the distance between current federal regulation of primaries and federalization of the whole process is wide enough that the constitutional issue is certain to be pressed in some quarters.[10]

If we set aside the legal issue relating to nationalization and turn to its policy implications, the strongest argument that proponents are apt to make in favor of this approach is that it is the only method that offers a reasonable assurance that a plan can in fact be implemented exactly as devised. With the other sources of authority—the national parties and the states—there are limits to their capacity to coordinate and effectively execute any plan. Only with federal legislation, where the jurisdiction can cover the entire nation and where the sovereignty is indisputable, can a clear plan be guaranteed of execution, if not success. If Congress enacts the legislation, it will in fact come into operation.

Proponents of nationalization also argue that nationalization can best ensure uniformity—for example, in methods of apportioning the allocation of delegates—and prevent harmful competition among the states for comparative advantages, such as holding the first contest. Just as states sometimes vie for certain economic benefits to the detriment of all, so they strive for more influence in the nominating system to the disadvantage of the fairness and legitimacy of the entire electoral process.

Those who have qualms about any plans for nationalization will no doubt point first to the fact that any such move begins to "incorporate" parties as official state agencies rather than private or semi-private associations. As parties lose their private status, they may also lose their integrity as viable associations. Where regulation has proceeded to excessive lengths in some states, as it once did in Wisconsin, the incorporated organizations simply died and the "real" parties formed once again as private associations outside the legal structure. If there is something to the general idea that political parties, as links between the people and the government, must retain a partially private status, then regulating their nominating rules by federal law might be a move in the wrong direction.

Nationalization plans differ, of course, in the extent to which they would *now* assert control over the entire process. But the passage of any plan, it can reasonably be argued, would establish the precedent that all the problems and issues of nominating politics must be brought before Congress and settled by national law. Legislators should consider not only the immediate consequences of the particular action but also the long-term effects on fundamental power relations and jurisdictional authority. Some possible consequences of a shift in jurisdictional authority to Congress would be a weakening of state and local parties and increasing pressures to ensure uniformity in all areas—for example, on rules relating to apportioning delegates, on laws establishing open or closed primaries, and eventually on methods of registration.

Perhaps the least likely, but the most dangerous, potential consequence of nationalization would be a violation of the doctrine of the separation of powers. With the power to determine the method of presidential nominations in its hands, Congress might change or adjust those procedures to help certain candidates or to set implicit conditions on presidents. There is sometimes the need to readjust the legislation—as in campaign finance legislation—and at such moments "political" motives are likely to be considered. Although struggles for advantage now go on in the national parties and in state legislatures, this is a different matter altogether from concentrating the power—and the conflict—in the legislative process. If Congress acquired this power, total control of the methods and procedures of the minority party would be at the discretion of the party controlling the Congress and the presidency.

Finally, the reverse side of the benefit of uniformity in nationalization is the benefit of diversity. With different authorities determining delegate selection rules, there is the opportunity for experimentation and for subsequent adjustment and readjustment. The national parties maintain independent control over their own organizations, and each of the states can try its own approach to mandating delegates—where the national parties permit—without having to worry about its effects on the entire system. Such experiments are far too risky under a uniform system. (Recall, however, that not all federal plans favor immediate uniformity.) Along the same lines, there is some benefit in "burying" certain issues that might not be resolved easily if fought out on the basis of clear principles. For example, on questions such as the participation of independents in primaries, it might be just as well that this issue is *not* raised to a matter of principle but is instead left to the separate struggles of different legislatures and settled according to the particular traditions and political alignments in each state.

The National Parties

National parties can legislate on the nominating process today by two different methods. First, they can divest themselves of authority they now have asserted, turning over a whole range of matters back to the states and state parties to decide. Second, they can assert more authority and adopt binding rules on the state and state parties in an effort to compel them to take certain specified steps. Since the first of these strategies returns power to the states, it is better discussed in the next section. Our concern at this point will be with the properties of further binding rules issued by the national parties.

Basically, there are three interrelated issues with respect to the national parties' ability to establish rules designing and controlling the delegate selection process: (1) the legal status of national party rules; (2) the ability of the parties to devise a general strategy and to enforce specific rules; and (3) the willingness of the parties to engage in the process of legislating.

The legal status of the parties in this area is a matter that has already been discussed. State parties cannot compel the national parties to accept state laws for delegate selection, but the national parties can control the seating of delegates at the convention, which puts them in a potential position to force states to comply with their rules under the threat of losing representation if they refuse. The parties have not, however, pushed this power to the limit, and part of the reason might be a reluctance to test their full legal authority. Suppose, for example, that the national parties sought to force states to hold—or not to hold—primaries. Would the courts acquiesce in this degree of national party power? Past precedents do not settle this question.

The experience of the Democratic party over the past decade provides grounds for evaluating the effectiveness of national parties in enforcing their plans and rules. During the initial stages of reform, when the McGovern–Fraser Commission's mandate to legislate was itself unclear, there was much controversy in the party between the reformers and party regulars. Notwithstanding its dubious legal position and all the talk of resistance, the commission achieved a rather remarkable rate of compliance: At the 1972 convention, forty states were judged in full compliance and ten others in substantial compliance. Since that time, the idea of "legislation" by national commissions under convention mandates and national committee supervision has been clearly endorsed by the conventions and in the new Democratic party charter. The party has also established an enforcement mechanism for compliance review that has begun to build its own extensive procedures and body of precedent. With the backing of the convention and with this new enforcement machinery, the national party has been able to legislate such major changes as proportional representation and delegate quotas.

Yet if these results provide a basis for confidence in this method, others raise serious questions. The basic course of development of the nominating process since 1968 may be the best example. Reformers claim that the intention of the McGovern–Fraser Commission's guidelines was *not* to increase the number of primaries but simply to eliminate the procedural irregularities in the caucuses. The results, however, were quite different. Perhaps the problem here was only one of miscalculation, but it might also have reflected the reformers' perception of the limits of what the party could accomplish where it did not have plenary power to legislate. Lacking this power—or unwilling to assume the risks of asserting it—the party left the states with the critical decision of whether or not to hold primaries.

By the same token, because the national party cannot compel a state legislature to adopt any particular kind of primary, its ultimate method of enforcement is indirect—to deny representation to delegates chosen in violation of the rules and to "require" the state party to select delegates in a party-run process. This method of enforcement sets up conflicts between the national party and the states, and in 1980 in a number of cases, it was the Democratic national party that gave in. The record of compliance thus far *has* been impressive, but the difficulties of enforcement may effectively curtail further extensions of the power.

The willingness of the national parties to undertake any major new initiatives is the final issue that must be examined in considering legislation by the national parties. The assertion of such power by the national parties represents a vast extension of their influence into areas formerly under the jurisdiction of the states and state parties. While Democrats have accepted the wisdom of this whole enterprise, Republicans have by and large rejected it. Of course, this simplifies the issue somewhat, as there has been some resistance to the process in the Democratic party, and Republicans in the last decade have enacted a few binding rules of their own, for example, a ban on ex officio delegates and a prohibition of proxy voting.[11] Overall, however, Republicans now seem to believe that a national party is structured best when the basic rules for delegate selection are set by the states and the state parties.

The difficulty facing Republicans, of course, is that while they have respected the concept of state sovereignty, the Democrats have not, and as a result, the Republican process in many primary states has been rewritten by Democrats. Republicans, if they prefer different rules than the Democrats, can attempt to fight this challenge in one of two ways—(1) by writing national party rules that *ban* rules that the Democrats pass but that Republicans disapprove of or (2) by attempting to get states to pass laws that accomplish the interests of local Republicans. The first of these alternatives is one that Republicans have thus far not pursued and probably rejected; the second is one that they have begun to work on, as evidenced by the increased number of states that have adopted substantially different delegate selection rules governing each of the parties.

The national parties face a further practical problem in legislating delegate selection rules: their sovereign bodies—the conventions—meet only once every four years. Unless they already have granted broad discretionary power to a party commission or to the national committee in advance—something that only Democrats have done so far—the time between recommendations and enactment can be more than four years.

Clearly, if the national parties were faced with the prospect of a national primary plan that might usurp their control, they might be willing to act together to protect their mutual interest in maintaining their autonomy, if necessary by means of legislating very explicit national party rules. Presumably, if leaders in both parties could agree on a basic plan, each party might then be willing to risk greater action without fearing that the plan would be undercut by state legislators from the opposing party.

State Governments and State Parties

Prior to 1900, the state parties had almost total control over the delegate selection process. During the Progressive era, some state governments stepped in and assumed part or all of the control by adopting primaries or by regulating party selection processes. From the Progressive era until the recent reforms, the state governments along with the state parties were recognized as the principal sources of sovereignty over delegate selection, with the state governments having the prerogative to preempt the state parties. Now, both the states and the state parties face a whole series of rules from the national parties that limit their discretion. The states still retain control over the critical issue of whether to hold primaries, but—at least in the case of the Democratic party—the character of both the primaries and the caucuses is tightly regulated by national party rules.

The great problem with attempting to use the states and state parties as the vehicle for change today is that of coordination. Because the states act on their own, according to any number of individual considerations, it would seem almost impossible to institute a plan in the strict sense by relying on state or state party action. Nevertheless, legislators for the nominating process might have some ideas of what the states and state parties will tend to do on their own or what they might tend to do if given certain powers and encouraged to take certain kinds of action. For example, if states were permitted to choose a specified number of their delegates ex officio, there are strong reasons to think that many of them would take advantage of this opportunity. At least for certain objectives, then, a national "plan" could be implemented by giving authority back to the states and relying on them to initiate the changes. Such a process for change might allow a consensus for a new approach to presidential nominations to emerge gradually, with the possibility of incremental changes being made by the states over a number of years. Many of the present conflicts would be decentralized and decided on a piecemeal and pluralist basis within the states.

If using the states and state parties to legislate poses some problems of coordination, it has the advantage of simplicity. For over fifty years now, the legal issues relating to the role of the states and state parties as legislators of the delegate selection process have had a chance to be worked out, and a stable set of expectations about power relationships has emerged. To the extent that the states can accomplish the objectives being sought, they therefore may be the best instruments to employ, although attaining certain objectives, such as limiting the length of the primary campaign, may be beyond the capacity of uncoordinated state action. Furthermore, the recent history of centralization of authority in the national Democratic party is a fact that has created new realities. So many changes already have taken place as a result of this centralization that, paradoxically, the states might now need certain national party rules to induce them to exercise more power.

Finally, relying on the states and state parties to control more of the decision would reverse the recent trend of transforming the parties into centralized entities run by national party commissions. Apart from the exact content of any changes that might be made, a shift to greater authority for the states would mark a return to the value of federalism in our party structure. Such a change would require a greater tolerance for diversity in the laws and practices of different states, with the national parties reserving their authority for a few areas, such as nondiscrimination or affirmative action provisions. Legislators, especially in the Democratic party, would have to be prepared at least implicitly to give up the quest for unitary practices in exchange for the advantages of a more federal approach.

DIRECTIONS OF CHANGE

More Direct Democracy

The two major proposals for increasing the degree of direct democracy in the nominating process both involve initiatives from federal legislation. They are the direct national primary with a run-off and a system of mandatory regional primaries in which all states would have to participate. The direct primary proposal has several variants. Senator Lowell Weicker recently introduced one such plan (S. 16). The main provisions of the Weicker legislation are:

- A national primary held on the first Tuesday of August in each presidential election year. Voters registered in their states by party affiliation vote only in the primary of their own party. Independents vote in the primary of their choice.

- If any candidate receives over 50 percent of the vote in the primary election, that candidate will be the nominee; otherwise, there will be a run-off between the top two vote recipients in the first round.

- Candidates qualify for a place on the ballot by submitting petitions having the names of at least 1 percent of the total vote in the last presidential election. Signatures by voters who are members of a different party would be invalid.

- Federal financing for primaries would be eliminated, and campaign contributions and expenditures are limited to the calendar year of the election.

The mandatory regional primary also has several variants. A typical plan, based on features selected from a number of different proposals,[12] contains the following major characteristics:

- The states and territories are divided into five regions. Primaries would be held beginning on the second Tuesday in March and thereafter the second Tuesday of each succeeding month through July.

- The order of the primaries would be determined by a lottery held by the Federal Election Commission prior to each primary date.
- Delegates are allocated on the basis of proportional representation from the statewide preference vote, with each candidate obtaining more than 5 percent of the vote being guaranteed a share of the delegates.
- The delegates, who must be approved by the candidate to whom they are pledged, are required to vote for their candidate for two ballots or until the candidate's share of the convention votes falls below 20 percent or until the candidate releases them.
- Candidates are placed on the ballots by the Federal Election Commission, which compiles a list of all generally recognized candidates. A candidate not on the list may petition in each region.

While both of these plans increase the degree of direct democracy, they obviously take very different approaches. The direct national primary would do away with the party convention as a mechanism for choosing presidential nominees, although conventions would be held after the primary to write the platforms and select the vice-presidential candidates. The regional primary plan, on the other hand, would retain the convention as the formal decisionmaking body for the nominations. While the voters would choose among national candidate preferences on the ballot (and not individual delegates), their preferences would be translated into proportional delegate shares. The use of delegates under the regional plan leads to another difference: whereas the national primary plan counts one person's vote equally with another's, the regional plan still allows the national parties to apportion delegates among the states, thus creating slight deviations from the standard of perfect democracy.

Clearly, the major difference between the two plans is the manner in which they would break a deadlock. The national primary plan uses a run-off, while the regional plan relies on the convention. Under the current system, as we have seen, the convention has not performed this function for some time, largely because the primary process as currently arranged narrows the field of candidates and allows a winner to be chosen before the convention. Curiously, proponents of the regional primary plan give little indication of whether their plan is *designed* to increase the likelihood that conventions will in fact have to make the decision. The plan could have this effect because it decreases the number of dates on which primaries are held, thereby giving the weaker candidates a chance to win more delegates before they are "forced" to withdraw from the race. Yet the silence of the regional primary advocates on this possibility suggests that they do not take it very seriously and that they envision no greater role for the convention under their plan than it plays under the present system. They may well be correct, as the effect noted above could be very slight. The pressure would still be substantial for candidates who did not do well in the first or second primary not only to drop out of the race but also to release their delegates. Even if the candidate who was victorious in the final rounds did not have a majority of the pledged delegates, the nomination decision might still be all but determined by the primary results.

In looking at the arguments that have been made on behalf of the plans for direct democracy since 1911, one notices that there has been a very remarkable shift in emphasis since the recent reforms. Prior to 1968, advocates of direct democracy based their case on essentially the same grounds as reformers. They claimed their plans would reduce the influence of party organizations, open up the process to different candidates, and increase the likelihood that the nominees would stand for distinct positions. None of these points is now raised by the advocates of more direct democracy because the current reforms already have carried out the kinds of institutional changes that were supposed to accomplish these objectives. The discretion of the conventions is now limited and the power of party leaders curtailed, if not completely eliminated.

Advocates of more direct democracy must therefore base their case today on quite different grounds. Their main argument now rests on the assertion that their plans would erase the procedural inequities of the current system and eliminate some of its undesirable effects, such as the excessive length of the active phase of the campaigns. Ironically, some of the objectives now sought by direct democracy advocates are precisely the ones that proponents of representative decisionmaking now favor. Advocates of direct democracy now put much less emphasis on the sanctity of the principles of openness and democracy and more emphasis on the alleged benefits in performance of their plans. Their argument is simply stated: more democracy will produce better results, improving on a democratic system that does not work very well.

The views of the proponents and opponents of these plans for more direct democracy need to be analyzed in terms of the five criteria for the nominating process outlined in the previous chapter. The discussion in some cases can be very brief, however, as the characteristics of the direct democracy plans would probably not differ materially from those of the current system.

1. *Legitimacy.* Advocates of direct democracy claim that their plans are based on the strongest and most widely favored principle of legitimacy for presidential nominations. Indeed, Senator Weicker's direct primary plan seems to be as fair and democratic on procedural grounds as any partisan system that could be devised. Only a nonpartisan, democratic election with provision for a run-off would possibly seem more democratic on procedural grounds. The regional primary plan is, of course, not perfectly democratic, but it deviates only slightly from that standard while maintaining the benefit of the convention. Moreover, unlike the current system, it provides an equal chance for the people of each region to have a first say, since the order of the primaries is determined by a lottery.

Advocates of more direct democracy base their case not only on principle, however, but on predicted performance. The direct democracy plan, they claim, would eliminate many of the de facto impediments to democracy found under the current system. Voter participation would increase because the caucus methods would be abolished and because the entire primary process would become more readily comprehensible to the citizenry. Independents also would be eligible to vote. Moreover, the reduction of the number of primary dates in the sequence under the regional plan and the elimination of the sequence altogether under the national primary plan would tend to increase turnout, as the results of competitive contests would not be decided before voters had the opportunity to exercise their franchise. Finally, the power of the news media under these plans would be reduced because there would be fewer opportunities for the media to interpret the results of electoral contests.

Opponents of these plans do not dispute the claim that participation under these plans would increase, probably by more under the national primary plan than under the regional plan. Yet participation in the form of voting turnout is not, in the view of many, the most important criterion for judging the effectiveness of a nominating system. Nor can one be certain that the outcome of any electoral contest among more than two choices will be representative of the voters' true intent, even with the provision of a run-off. Under the national primary plan, the winners of the first round might be choices from the two polar ideological wings within a party, for example, George Wallace and George McGovern in the Democratic party in 1972. The candidates in the middle, who would probably include in their number the person having the greatest chance of commanding a majority in a run-off, would be eliminated from the race altogether.

Another problem with these plans is that they would diminish the effective influence of certain geographically based minorities, especially blacks. This result follows from the fact that most delegates are now selected from constituencies at the congressional district level or below, with the number of delegates allotted to these districts based on the combined criteria of population and turnout in *general* elections. What this means is that the size of a district's delegation is not affected by the number of voters who turn out for the primary. Districts dominated by groups that turn out at low rates in primaries are thus able to maintain much of their influence, assuming, of course, that the delegates who are chosen can be presumed to "speak for" all their constituents. Relative to the factor of total primary turnout alone, then, the residents of these districts are overrepresented to an appreciable extent.[13] The plans for more direct democracy would eliminate this bonus—the regional primary because it bases the allocation of delegates on statewide totals and the direct primary plan because each person's vote counts exactly the same as another's. While both of these plans are certainly "fairer" than the current system by all of the criteria of strict democracy, they would diminish the influence of groups that proponents of direct democracy usually claim they want to protect.

The assertion that these plans eliminate the problems related to sequence under the current system makes sense only in the case of the national primary proposal. It is true, of course, that under the regional plan each region is fairly treated in the sense of having an equal chance to come first. This modest benefit aside, however, it remains that once the order of primaries in any given year has been determined, what follows may be just as irrational as that which exists under the present system. For example, it hardly would help a candidate from the West at the prime of his career if his region turns up fourth and fifth in the two elections in which he competes. Much more important, however, is the question of whether strict regional groupings would eliminate, as distinct from actually creating, a bias. Because regions do have distinct political characteristics in terms of voting behavior, it seems that any sequential arrangement based on region produces a very significant bias in any given year. The lottery will not eliminate this bias but only make its character random from one election to the next. Indeed, if one wanted to eliminate a bias, the fairest system, given a sequential arrangement, would be one in which the states holding primaries on the same day are drawn from *different* regions. There are, to be sure, some sensible reasons for regional grouping that have to do with voter interest, the candidates' travel schedules, convenience for the media, and the like, but these considerations are very different from any claim that a regional primary plan would eliminate a sequential bias.

The regional primary plan maintains the party conventions. A great deal of emphasis is placed on ensuring that delegates will reflect the preferences of the voters, but almost no consideration is given to the question of who the delegates are. This presents no problem if the nomination decision is made on the first ballot, which may ordinarily be the case, but if the convention does have to make the decision, it is questionable whether delegates selected without regard to their own standing—indeed virtually hand-picked by the candidates—are well-suited to perform this task. The public might well find a convention of this sort highly objectionable. By attempting to ensure democratic legitimacy in the selection of delegates, regional primary advocates may have created problems in legitimacy for the convention.

Finally, on the issue of news media influence, it is difficult to make predictions with any confidence. The regional primary plan might reduce the news media's power as it derives from interpreting contests—both because there would be fewer events to interpret and because the latitude that comes from analyzing results in small states very early in the race would be eliminated. Both these changes, however, appear to be only marginal, and a dramatic change in the media's role is difficult to imagine.

The impact of the national primary in reducing news media influence might seem, by this reasoning, very substantial, for there would be no actual electoral contest to interpret before the choice is made (or one contest, in the event that a run-off is required). Recall, however, that news media influence derives not only from their role in interpreting electoral results but also from their ability to shape perceptions about the candidates and the campaign *before* any real contest has yet taken place.

What the media might lose in their interpretive powers under a national primary, they could therefore gain in "shaping" powers. The national primary is the plan that provides the media with the greatest possible influence in shaping events, since everything hinges on one contest and no actual results from any previous contest exist to check trends of reporting. As Austin Ranney has argued:

> In a national primary . . . the only pre-election facts relevant to who was winning would be public opinion polls and estimates of the sizes of crowds at public meetings . . . neither constitutes hard data in the sense that election returns do. . . . Thus, a one-day national direct primary would give the news media even more power than they now have to influence the outcomes of contests for nominations by shaping most people's perceptions of how these contests were proceeding.[14]

2. *Character of the Candidates.* The more democratic systems apparently would reduce the chances of the success of insurgents and outsiders in comparison with the current system. The sequenced series, we have seen, now allows the outsider to put an immense share of time and limited campaign resources into one or two small states where such an investment has a real chance of paying off. Doing well in one of these contests can then serve to launch a candidate's national campaign. Under the regional primary proposal, the expanded size of the constituency of the first contest would take away part of this advantage to the outsider. Even more important, the selection of the first primary date by lottery only seventy days in advance would make it impossible for any candidate to know where to begin in advance. By expanding the size of the constituency to the entire nation, the national primary plan might make it even more difficult for insurgents. As two prominent scholars have argued: "Established, well-known politicians would have an even stronger advantage over spokesmen for new groups and new ideas than they have had."[15]

This predicted effect could be negated, however, by the role of the media in a regional or especially a national primary. By the use of preelection polls, an artificial sequence could in effect be created, with a great deal of publicity going to the candidates rising in the polls. A new form of a national image or insurgency campaign might therefore take hold—even without the current string of separate primaries. What Charles Guggenheim said of the role of the media under the current system could also be true under a national primary plan:

> There's a phenomenon in American politics which television has emphasized: Men who have no record are often more appealing than men who have a record. . . . TV dramatizes this political virginity. Before there was television, an unknown couldn't run at all because he couldn't get the exposure. With television, he can become known in a very short time.[16]

It is interesting to observe reactions to statements about the relative bias of the nominating system to outsiders. When the issue is stated in terms of eliminating institutional arrangements that create advantages for the outsider, many people readily approve. Indeed, a number of advocates of more direct democracy now press this argument, which puts them in the curious position of favoring a more democratic system in order to help the more establishment candidates. When the issue is posed in terms of assisting well-known figures (and favoring them chiefly because they are well-known), however, many object on the grounds that the public then would not have sufficient time to see candidates tested and that the entire selection process would be transformed into a mere popularity contest.

This dilemma of either favoring outsiders or promoting popular figures appears on first analysis to be endemic to the nominating process itself. Many observers, however, doubt that the dilemma is anything more than a function of the choice between the alternatives of the present system and the national primary. Under other nominating systems, these two problems would not be aspects of a single trade-off, but separable issues that could be handled independently. In other words, there can be systems that give neither an undue benefit to the outsider nor too much of an advantage to mere popularity. Defenders of the regional primary plan undoubtedly would argue that their plan succeeds in this respect, or at the very least strikes a better balance than the current system or the direct national primary. Advocates of greater representation, as we shall see, make the same claim.

3. *Candidate Behavior* and 4. *Controlling Choice and Change.* Since the current system and both the proposals for more direct democracy involve the same basic strategy of going to the public to win the

nomination, there would appear to be no major differences among them in respect to their impact on candidate behavior or controlling choice and change. It may well be, as we have just seen, that the more democratic systems would give less weight to insurgency, thus having the second-order consequence of inducing prospective aspirants to make a reputation for themselves before they run for office; and it is conceivable that the national direct primary might, by favoring established figures, promote a degree of resistance to change when compared with the current system. Indeed, these very possibilities have led some so-called moderates to reduce their opposition to a direct national primary, believing that it might be the lesser of two evils.[17] When all is said and done, however, these systems are all basically democratic and all put the attribute of popular leadership at the center of the whole process. Given this fundamental similarity, the differences that might arise among them on second-order consequences like candidate behavior and the system's influence on choice and change must be matters more of speculation than anything else. Most attempts to draw conclusions here would be little more than exercises in creative writing.

Advocates of more direct democracy insist that their plan will significantly reduce the length of the active campaign. Under the regional primary plan, the date of the first contest would be moved up to the first Tuesday in March (or April under some proposals), which would mean a marginal change from the January 21 opening date of the 1980 caucus in Iowa. The main incentive to shorten the campaign under the regional plan, however, comes less from the date on which the first primary is scheduled than from the device of the lottery that selects the region to lead off the series. Until the lottery takes place (seventy days before the first primary), none of the candidates knows the specific region in which to begin campaigning. The lottery day is thus intended to mark the official opening of the campaign and to set a date before which campaign activity would be neither interesting to the American people nor very effective for the candidates. Under the direct primary plan of Senator Weicker, an attempt is made to shorten the campaign by preventing the candidates from accepting any campaign contributions prior to the start of the calendar year of the election and, more significantly, by holding off the time of the primary election all the way until August.

Whether and to what extent either of these proposals actually would reduce the length of the active campaign is difficult to say.

The level of interest in the campaign would be influenced to a limited extent under any sequential arrangement of primaries by the date of the first contest. Attempting to extrapolate from this experience to behavior under a national primary, however, is very questionable, and if Senator Weicker's plan would work in this respect, he would face the problem of having the campaign peak during the height of the vacation season. For the most part, however, neither of these plans touches the two major factors that, viewed from a comparative and historical perspective, govern the length of the campaign. First, the date of elections in America is set by calendar and not by the discretion of governing officials, as is the case under a parliamentary system. All the candidates therefore know exactly when the electoral season will take place, and the American electoral clock is set to a four-year pace. Second, the general constituency that chooses the nominee is now known in advance: It is, in some form, the public. As long as candidates know that the final decision regarding the nomination is made by the people, some of them undoubtedly will find it to their advantage to begin their active public campaigning very early, and the media will begin covering the campaign just as soon as the story becomes interesting. If this is the case, the only real deterrent to the long public campaign is to change the authority that decides the nominee. By this means, the candidates' *incentive* to campaign in the present fashion would decline, and the news media would have to look elsewhere for their stories.

5. *Effects on Governing.* Except for remarking on some of the negative effects of the length of the campaign on the leadership of an incumbent president, advocates of more direct democracy in the nominating system have had very little to say about the potential consequences of their plans for the governing process. Perhaps this silence follows from the fact that advocates of these plans see little or no essential difference between their plans and the current system—and this assessment may well be correct. If the current system leaves little discretion to parties, however, and if through its individualistic and plebiscitary campaigns it encourages the idea of the president as a public opinion leader, it probably can be said that the direct democracy plans go even further in these same directions. Under both plans, although especially under the national primary plan, the very concept of the political party appears to be threatened.

In the case of the regional primary plan, none of the delegates is anything other than a simple messenger. No special incentives are created under this system for the candidates to enter into a working arrangement with other elites in the party, and no special ties are encouraged between the presidential candidates and the members of their own party in Congress. Under the direct national primary plan, even the pretense to negotiation is dropped, and the nominating decision is given over to the electorate. It is true, of course, that the role of parties is already quite limited under the present system, and in this respect, neither of the two plans may mark a radical departure from the status quo. For those concerned about maintaining or reviving parties, however, adoption of either of these plans would make that task much more difficult.

Rationalizing the Status Quo

A second group of plans involves maintaining essentially the same degree of direct democracy that we currently have, but attempting to bring the system into some kind of order. One of the simplest plans was introduced by two congressmen with diametrically opposed political viewpoints but with the common experience of having run for their party's nomination and lost: Morris K. Udall (Democrat, Arizona) and John Ashbrook (Republican, Ohio).[18] While not requiring any state to adopt a primary, the plan would limit the time when primaries could be held and standardize them. Its specifics are as follows:

- Any state deciding to have a primary must hold it on one of four dates: the second Tuesday in March, April, May, or June of the presidential year.

- The Federal Election Commission would compile a list of candidates for president who would be included on the ballots of each state. Additional candidates could be included by petition on any state ballot.

- States holding primaries would be required to adopt a presidential preference format and allocate delegates in proportion to the candidates' share of the votes. Candidates receiving more than 10 percent of the vote would be guaranteed delegate representation.

The main objectives of this plan are to shorten the campaign, eliminate the unfair advantage for the states currently holding contests early in the year, and standardize and simplify the primary rules. The plan would change the nominating system in many of the same ways as the regional primary proposal, except that it would not create the peculiar effects of regionalism or keep everyone in suspense until a lottery determined the order of the primaries. States choosing to hold primaries would have the option of picking their own date among the four possibilities. This flexibility could create a problem, however, as most states probably would select the first or the last primary date in order to maximize their influence.

A second plan for rationalizing the current system is to have the national parties set dates before and after which primaries and caucuses could not be held. Although this plan would not standardize the primary rules any more than under the present system, it could significantly change the current sequential pattern if the campaign season were limited to a shorter period. For example, if the contests were limited to a three-month period from April through June, it would be highly unlikely that any state would have a primary date at the beginning all to itself. The plan has the obvious advantage of simplicity at the same time that it avoids the problems of national regulation, but it faces the difficulties of coordination between the national parties and enforcement of national party rules against the wishes of the states. The Democratic party, in fact, has already begun to implement this kind of plan and has met with some resistance. In 1980, a national party rule set March 11 and June 10 as the opening and closing dates for the delegate selection season, but a number of states demanded and were granted exemptions.

The final proposal to rationalize the current system is an optional regional primary plan favored by Senator Robert Packwood (Republican, Oregon).[19] This plan has the same basic rules as the mandatory regional plan, except that it gives the states the choice of whether they wish to hold a primary. As long as most states continue to have primaries, the plan would probably have the same consequences as the mandatory regional plan. To induce the states to retain their primaries, Packwood's plan would use federal funds to reimburse the states for the costs of holding a primary. One minor problem, not perhaps foreseen in the legislation, is the possibility that some states would decide on whether or not to hold a primary on the basis of when their region was scheduled by the lottery.

Increasing the Role of Representative Decisionmaking

All too often those seeking institutional change lose sight of their basic objectives and concentrate their energies on achieving certain specific procedural changes. The link between these changes and their objectives may once have been considered, but as time goes on, proponents of change may fail to reassess their position, allowing their procedural goals to become ends in themselves. Today, advocates of representative decisionmaking must avoid falling into a similar trap. It would be all too easy to assume that since the current system has developed chiefly as a result of the increase in the number of primaries, all that would need to be done to restore representative decisionmaking is reduce the number of primaries. Perhaps this might work; yet from what we have seen about changing campaign practices within caucus states and from the changes in the caucus rules themselves, this solution might fall short of achieving a desirable representative process and might not be the best means to accomplish that end.

In order to keep the relationship between procedural goals and objectives clearly in focus, the objectives must be defined in a reasonably concrete fashion. In the case of decisionmaking by direct democracy, the objectives were almost self-evident and needed no explanation: Direct democracy seeks to have the people choose the nominees and to have each person's vote count the same as everyone else's. In the case of a representative decisionmaking process, however, the meaning is not so clear, and a definition of representation in this context needs to be formulated before specific plans can be discussed.

In formal terms, a representative decisionmaking body (process) is one in which the representatives—or a sufficient number of them—retain discretion so that the body's decisions are not dictated by those who select the representatives but remain under the purview of the representatives themselves, acting either individually or in groups. Put more simply, the representative process is one that retains the capacity to make a choice through deliberation and bargaining. By this definition, it is clear that modern conventions remain representative bodies in respect to platform and rules questions but that they are not representative bodies in respect to the nominating decision.

This definition, while useful as a starting point for discussion, is too formal to be helpful in practice. For example, exactly what "retaining discretion" means in a practical sense for a delegate is unclear. A nominating convention is not the usual kind of representative body charged with making a variety of decisions over a wide range of issues. On the contrary, it meets for one major purpose—choosing a presidential nominee. To compare it, therefore, to a legislative body or to equate the delegate's role with that of the legislative representative is to confuse the practical issue more than to clarify it. Unlike the representative, the delegate has one main decision to make, and unlike most decisions that the representative faces, the delegate's decision is one about which many citizens will have a decided and easily expressed view, that is, candidate X should be the party's nominee. Under these circumstances, citizens selecting the delegates will sometimes, if not usually, make an attempt to bind delegates in their vote, whether formally or informally. And while there is a difference in the binding power of formal instructions embodied in rules or laws and informal instructions made during the course of the selection process, informal instructions still can be powerful enough in practice to eliminate discretion from the nominating decision. Accordingly, a nominating process that maintained the formal discretion of the delegates might not in practice realize the objective of representative decisionmaking. Indeed, today, when candidate organizations are active throughout the nation in lining up delegates, relying on formal changes in the delegate's role *alone* might prove ineffective.

The earlier definition of a representative decisionmaking process may also be too stringent, at least for many advocates of representation today. Because the nature of the representative act in this instance is to make only one major decision, some believe that it would be unreasonable to expect the convention always to have effective discretion. Many of the advocates of a representative process today are seeking not a guarantee of a representative decisionmaking process but rather a situation in which it is likely to occur under certain circumstances. This formulation is usually expressed in such terms as: where none of the candidates is the overwhelming favorite of the rank and file, the nominating process should allow representatives to choose the nominees. In other words, many advocates of representation today are not completely opposed to direct democracy. They favor instead a balance between the principles of direct democracy and representative decisionmaking.

The practical nature of these objections to the original definition of a representative decisionmaking process makes the task of revising it along precise lines very difficult. Rather than straining for more exactitude than is possible, however, it makes sense to give a looser definition, even including the imprecisions. A representative nominating process, we can then say, would have two characteristics (and some might not even insist on the first): (1) It would always maintain at least the theoretical option to exercise discretion on the nominating decision, and (2) it would, in fact, promote a discretionary decision process when no one candidate is a clear favorite of the rank and file.

In considering how to achieve the objective of a representative decisionmaking process, two basic strategies come to mind. Under the first, an effort would be made to increase the probability that delegates will in fact enter the process with discretion. The steps to be taken here might involve reducing the number of formally bound delegates and, through a variety of techniques, increasing the probability that formally unbound delegates will have both the personal standing and the incentive to exercise discretion. The second basic strategy involves attempting to maintain as much diversity as possible in the delegates' representation of candidate preferences. The logic here is simple: If there is no absolute majority among delegates chosen to reflect candidate preferences, then the process automatically will be thrown into a discretionary situation. Under this strategy, steps would be taken to discourage any artificial winnowing of the list of possible candidates prior to the choice of all the delegates and to ensure that candidate preferences expressed by citizens are not lost along the way. These general strategies may be outlined as follows:

Strategy 1
Increase Initial Delegate Discretion

1. Elect delegates as individuals, not formally bound to any national candidate preference. *Reason*: Delegates who are not bound formally by law are more likely to exercise discretion.

2. Choose more delegates by caucuses than primaries. Eliminate rules that bind caucus delegates to national candidate preferences. *Reason*: Delegates chosen in caucuses are more likely to exercise discretion than those elected in a primary, as they represent local party interests.

3. Select delegates ex officio. *Reason*: Their choice as delegates then would be largely if not entirely unconnected with their candidate preference, and they might have the personal standing and interest to keep their options open until the process is under way.

4. Avoid an "untimely" selection of delegates—that is, the choice of delegates in years prior to the calendar year of the election. *Reason*: Delegates chosen before the campaign is under way cannot be bound easily, as circumstances are likely to change and as candidates have not yet declared or formed large organizations.

Strategy 2
Maintain Diversity in Representation of Candidate Preferences

1. Find the sequence that keeps possible winning candidates from dropping out before delegates are chosen; this means reducing the number of primary dates dramatically and concentrating primaries in a shorter time span. *Reason*: With more possible candidates winning more delegates, an initial majority for any one candidate is less likely.

2. Elect delegates, if being chosen individually, from smaller rather than larger constituencies. *Reason*: This will tend to maintain the most diversity among delegates in their candidate choice.

3. Select delegates by proportional representation with lower cut-off points. *Reason*: Diversity is maintained.

4. Bound delegates cannot be released by their candidate. *Reason*: This maintains diversity on the initial convention ballot.

These strategies are partially in tension; under the first, delegates are kept uncommitted to any national candidate, while under the second, they are committed in such a way as not to lose any potential diversity. There are ways, however, of combining the two strategies in one system, either by means of using aspects of the purest elements of each or compromising and mixing elements of both. The choice in such matters should not be based entirely on one's preference in principle for one strategy or another, but also on assessments of how well each would work in practice. For example, under any strategy that relies on maintaining the initial discretion of the delegate, the likelihood that such delegates will not in fact be informally bound when they are chosen must be considered.

Finally, it is important to remember that this discussion of strategies has been directed at the question of how to move the nominating system toward a representative decisionmaking process. What the discussion did not include is the question of what produces the right kind of representation. It would stretch the limits of common sense to make changes to guarantee a representative decisionmaking process if the representatives chosen lacked either the legitimacy to impose a decision or the competence to act prudently. Accordingly, whatever plan is proposed to promote a representative decisionmaking process must also be judged by the quality of its representation—by such criteria as whether the delegates are able to speak on behalf of the rank and file, whether they possess the qualities of good judgment, and whether they are put into a setting in which they have the opportunity to make an intelligent decision.

One plan for increasing the element of representative decisionmaking that relies predominantly on federal legislation has been offered by Jeane Kirkpatrick, currently America's ambassador to the United Nations. Kirkpatrick's plan would eliminate primaries altogether and have candidates selected by conventions made up *exclusively* of elected public officials and party leaders. In her words:

> I propose that Congress by national legislation provide that the nominating process of each party shall consist of its elected public officials and party leaders—its congressmen, senators, governors, state party chair and cochairs, mayors of major cities, and possibly members of the national committees. I propose that there be no presidential primaries at all.[20]

Only under such a system, Kirkpatrick argues, would the delegates have the discretion to exercise an informal choice about the candidates' capacity to govern. If primaries were permitted, they would inevitably constrain the delegates, notwithstanding any legal guarantees of discretion: "[A]ny input from the primaries would create a situation in which the elected public and party officials would be vulnerable to charges of illegitimacy if they did not reach a decision that was consistent with the outcome of whatever participatory process were devised."[21] Despite the absence of primaries, however, Kirkpatrick contends that her plan would be sufficiently broad based to pass the test of legitimacy, for the public and party officials have themselves been chosen in democratic election.

Kirkpatrick's plan is designed to produce the greatest possible degree of "peer review" and thereby to increase the probability of "producing a better set of nominees." But as she wonders herself,

"Is it feasible?" In eliminating altogether any popular input into the process, the plan boldly challenges some seventy years of tradition. One may wonder whether any politicians today are willing to go so far and whether such a change could meet the test of public legitimacy. Finally, the plan's reliance on federal legislation to be put into effect means further national regulation of political parties and risks altering their character as essentially private associations. The burden of changing or adjusting the plan would inevitably fall on Congress.

Another plan for increasing the element of representative decision-making that relies predominantly on federal legislation is the national primary day proposal developed by the political scientist Everett Ladd.[22] The main feature of the Ladd proposal is a nationally structured primary that would choose two-thirds of the delegates to the convention, with the other third being chosen by the parties and consisting almost entirely of ex officio delegates. The specifics are as follows:

- All states hold their primaries on the same day, for example, the third Tuesday in June. Delegates are allocated within the states on the basis of proportional representation for candidate preference. A low threshold, for example, 10 percent, is used as a guarantee for a share of the delegates.

- Delegates chosen in the primaries are bound to their candidate for one—and only one—ballot, regardless of whether the candidate withdraws or indicates support for someone else.

- Candidates qualify for the ballot through (1) certification by the National Committee of the party, based on a candidate's intentions and support or (2) by petition or X number of enrolled party members from at least twelve states.

- One-third of the delegates are chosen wholly outside the primaries. The following party members, which comprise most of that total, would be selected ex officio: senators, representatives, governors, the national chairman and cochairman, members of the National Committee, and the chairman and vice-chairman of each state party. These delegates, numbering on the order now of 1,000 to 1,200, would, of course, not be bound to any candidate. (The parties would adjust the total number of delegates to conform roughly with the proportion determined by the ex officio delegates.)

- The federal government gives each national party committee $15 million to spend in accordance with its designated purposes. This amount would be in addition to the public funding for the candidates.

This plan combines the principles of direct democracy and representative decisionmaking, attempting to give each its proper weight. The element of direct democracy is found in the primary that binds the delegates to a particular candidate preference. All party members or citizens—Ladd does not deal with the question of closed versus open primaries—would be able to express their preference on the same day. (This aspect of the plan is similar to the national primary proposal of Senator Weicker.) The elements of the plan encouraging representative decisionmaking are found first in the large number of delegates selected ex officio and, to a lesser extent, in the very democratic nature of the primary rules, which would tend to maintain as much diversity as possible in candidate preferences.

Ladd has devised what amounts to a sliding balance between these two principles. The better a candidate does in the democratic contest, the less support he would need from the ex officio delegates. As a practical matter, an extremely popular candidate, one winning 60 percent of the delegates from the primaries, probably would have little difficulty in securing enough support from the uncommitted delegates to win the nomination. As the popular contest becomes closer, however, the chances for genuine representative decisionmaking increase correspondingly. The convention could exercise discretion, taking into account not only the popular vote total in the primary but also other considerations.

Ladd is careful in his proposal to be concerned not only with forcing a representative decision but also with ensuring that the convention is well-suited to making a good choice. The mix of delegates from the primary and from officeholders and party officials would provide a broad base of support, muting any criticisms that the convention did not speak for the rank and file. At the same time, the ex officio delegates—mostly professional politicians—would bring a professional dimension in the assessment of the candidates, one based not only on how the candidates appear as popular leaders but also on how they look to their peers. Ladd's emphasis is also clearly on building the parties by giving party officials important roles in the selection of candidates. The idea that $15 million of public funding should go to the parties also promotes the strengthening of parties.

Ladd has devised a strikingly ingenious plan, combining the most extreme aspects of the two strategies presented earlier. His national primary proposal gives the plan a dimension of direct democracy that exceeds that which we have today. This democratic element sugar-coats the highly representative strategy of choosing nearly one-third of the delegates ex officio, a method that was banned by both parties in the party reforms of the early 1970s. Undoubtedly, the plan would be the subject of criticism from both sides—a possible indication of its balance. For all those who might attack it as undemocratic, it would have its defenders among advocates of representative decisionmaking.

Ladd's plan, however, can certainly be questioned on other grounds than whether it is too democratic or not democratic enough. Besides the serious objections to any plan initiated by Congress, a critic might wonder whether the plan is not in a sense *too* clever for its own good. Specifically, its democratic element is so clear and visible that it might conceivably put too much informal pressure on the representative process to do its bidding. Then, too, because the plan includes a single national primary, it raises—although it by no means simply succumbs to—some of the same problems as the simple national primary. Would too much weight, for example, be given under this plan to the mere popular figure? Would the plan, because it does mark such a radical departure from current methods, have unforeseen consequences? Finally, although the financing provisions are separable from the rest of the plan, the effect of more public financing might be to incorporate the parties further into the legal structure of the government, thereby perhaps establishing the claim for further public regulation. Any plan that aids the major parties must also come to grips with the problem of equity for minor parties.

Terry Sanford, a former governor of North Carolina as well as a former presidential aspirant, has offered a second and quite different plan to promote representative decisionmaking.[23] Sanford would rely on national party rules for the implementation of his plan, with the expectation that *both* parties would accept the same basic rules and that this agreement would quickly bring the state legislature and state parties into compliance. Sanford's plan follows the first strategy outlined above of attempting to increase the discretion for the delegates. His objective, as he states it, is to "send thinking delegates to the national convention."[24] The main features of his plan are:

- All delegates are chosen individually without any kind of formal commitment required.
- Delegates are chosen from single-member districts, whether by election in a primary or in a caucus. (Selection of a small number of ex officio delegates by state conventions or other processes also would be allowed.) Statements of candidate preference are not permitted on the ballot.
- Presidential primaries are still permitted, but they are only "beauty contests." Delegates would not be chosen or mandated by these primary results. Primaries would be held on any one of six dates in March and April, the state selecting its own date. No effort would be made to achieve regional groupings.

Under the Sanford plan, each delegate becomes, in essence, a full representative, selected on the basis of the confidence voters have in him, "just as we elect school board members, state representatives, and other public officials."[25] The choice of such delegates, where selected by election and not by caucuses, is fully democratic, but since the people do not have a direct voice in choosing the nominees, it is not direct democracy. (On the other hand, since Sanford envisions that most of the delegates will be chosen by election, the choice of the representatives is more democratic than under Ladd's proposal.) Where an element of direct democracy does come into play is in the (optional) primaries, where the popularity of the candidates can presumably be measured and taken into account as one factor in the delegates' decision.

Sanford is concerned not only with providing the delegates with discretion but also with encouraging them, through certain constitutional changes, to use their discretion wisely. Although Sanford probably believes that many of the delegates chosen through this process would be local party officials, he does not stress the fact that they already would be knowledgeable about all the candidates. Nor does he believe that this knowledge is best gained at the convention itself. He therefore proposes a series of state forums where the candidates would go before the chosen delegates to answer questions and debate the issues.

Sanford's plan, like Ladd's, would require extensive changes from the basic outline of the current nominating process. Whether the national parties could—or would—use their authority to implement

such a plan is questionable, although Sanford has no doubts about
the inherent power of the national parties to legislate the plan.
Whether the delegates chosen by this method would in fact possess
discretion is open to question. Difficult as it might be, well-organized
and well-financed national candidate campaigns might be able to
penetrate this process and convert these *de jure* uncommitted delegates into bound messengers. The success of this proposal would
depend, then, on whether the candidates found it so difficult to
select their own delegates that they would give up on the attempt,
choosing instead—as Sanford would like—to make an effort to deal
with the delegates after they were selected. While Sanford stresses
the quality of the delegates likely to be selected, it might be wondered whether the mass of delegates at the convention would not
resemble a group of well-intentioned amateurs, too proud to be
moved in blocs yet not knowledgeable enough about the candidates
to offer much hope of providing a real screen of the candidates by
seasoned professionals.

This completes a survey of the two major *full-scale* plans for implementing representative decisionmaking. But a *total* overhaul of
the form of the current system is not necessary to achieve the same
result. Proposals as simple—and as dramatic—as allowing the selection of up to 40 percent of each state's delegation ex officio might
work just as well.[26]

For example, this sort of proposal was suggested by the President's
Commission for a National Agenda for the Eighties, formed by President Carter after his "spiritual malaise" speech of July 17, 1979. The
commission report, which appeared in late 1980, stated:

> In light of the trend of weaker political parties, the Panel views processes to
> strengthen the parties as important steps in encouraging the coalition-building
> approach to decision making. Strong parties and party leadership can provide
> incentives for cooperation in policymaking. . . . [The panel recommends that]
> a certain percentage of the delegates at a party's Presidential nominating con-
> vention—perhaps one-fifth to one-third—should be set aside for a party's
> elected officeholders, major current and recent candidates, and its own offi-
> cers. This proposal is not intended to replace primaries, but merely to restore
> some balance to the current system, whereby party leaders have almost no
> influence over the selection of a party's presidential nominee.[27]

As noted, the commission's proposal emphasizes building coalitions, including greater cooperation and coordination between the
president and Congress. In addition, it calls for increased public par-

ticipation, peer review, the exercise of independent judgment by delegates, a means for shortening the primary season, and the implementation of these proposals by the political parties themselves. It should be noted that these ends simply may not be compatible.

The following is an elaboration of various individual steps that could be taken. As with the President's Commission's recommendations, some of these steps conflict with each other, but most do not. A plan for achieving representative decisionmaking could be assembled by arranging any number of these separate items into a single package.

1. *Reduce the Number of Primaries.* This change could happen by itself, without any national plan, as state legislatures reassess their laws. The national parties and a private commission might encourage such action merely by asking the states to reconsider their laws and by making a case for representative decisionmaking. Alternatively, as Donald Fraser has suggested, the national parties could attempt to restrict the number of primaries, setting a limit and choosing among states by some kind of lottery.[28]

2. *Devalue the Primaries.* This change could be made by allowing or encouraging states holding primaries to mandate only part of their delegations on the basis of the primary results. Alternatively, a national party rule could require that no more than X percent of the delegates in any state may be bound by primary results.[29]

3. *Allow an End to Proportional Representation.* The Democratic National Committee could remove its requirement for proportional representation, whether in primaries or caucuses or both. States then could decide how their delegates would be selected, moving to systems that give more discretion to the delegates. General guidelines respecting the size of constituencies could be maintained to avoid winner-take-all races at the statewide level. Alternatively, the parties could require the selection of unbound delegates as individuals.

4. *Allow Ex Officio Delegates.* The two parties could remove their ban on ex officio delegates and give the states the option to select a certain portion of their delegates by this method. Alternatively, the national parties could require the states to choose ex officio delegates as well as provide for some national ex officio delegates. To

minimize the danger of extremism in the event that party organizations become more ideological, the greater part of these ex officio delegates could be drawn from the ranks of elected officials—governors, mayors, and members of Congress.

5. *Untimely Selection of Delegates.* The Democratic party could remove its requirements for the timely selection of delegates, allowing a certain number of delegates to be chosen before the election year.

6. *Limitation of the Primary Season.* The primaries and caucuses held during the calendar election year could be confined to a number of fixed dates within a relatively brief time period, for example, from mid–April through mid–June. This plan could be enforced by congressional legislation or by national party rules, perhaps with the two national parties reaching some kind of working agreement.

7. *Lower Proportional Representation Cutoffs.* The Democratic national party could allow states choosing to use proportional candidate preference primaries to employ a cutoff figure below that now required. Alternatively, the party could require a lower cutoff, say of 10 or 15 percent in large districts.

These steps to increase the representative character of the convention involve a great number of options and leave unanswered the issue of the extent to which the national parties either should allow or require the states and state parties to adopt more discretionary delegate selection procedures. For those favoring greater federalism and diversity in party structure, the emphasis should be placed on *removing* current national party requirements and allowing states to proceed on their own, maintaining only those provisions ensuring access or affirmative action for various groups. Even for those favoring federalism, however, prudence might suggest the need for some national party action to encourage states to undo some of the things that national party action has forced them to do over the past decade. Increasing the degree of representative decisionmaking in the presidential selection process will have a number of consequences, which must be judged against the criteria outlined in the previous chapter.

1. *Legitimacy.* These plans would be attacked on the grounds that a representative decisionmaking process is not sufficiently democratic. Some of these plans or "packages" obviously would be more vulnerable to this charge than others. Proponents of representative decisionmaking therefore face the task, in varying degrees, of convincing the public that this method is legitimate. Such a defense could be made first on the grounds that representative decisionmaking is democratic, in that the popular choice requires deliberation and the consideration of second and third preferences. If this is the only defense of representation, however, its other classical justification—filtration of the public's demand—would be overlooked, and when the time came for delegates to exercise their discretion in a truly deliberative fashion, they might be afraid to do so. Accordingly, proponents of representative decisionmaking also must make at least the public argument that a representative process is desirable because it allows a deliberative body to act as a filter and make an independent choice on the basis of its assessment of the needs of the party and the nation. Today, obviously, defenders of representative processes must be certain that representatives are selected in a defensible manner, without procedural irregularities and with some access for the rank and file.

2. *Character of the Candidates.* Defenders of representation argue that their system normally would tend to close the doors to outsiders or insurgents, except in those rare instances in which the party itself becomes heavily influenced by an influx of new activist members. Yet if the choice is narrowed in this respect, it is not as narrow as it would be under the national primary plan, for the convention would not be limited to the popular favorite in a brokered situation. Most important, the representative process actually is more open than the current nominating process in one respect: It can turn to persons who, for whatever reason, do not become active candidates during the campaign. This capacity, some believe, is one of the greatest assets of a representative process.

3. *Candidate Behavior.* The full dimensions of change that would result in a representative decisionmaking process on this count are unknown. Almost certainly, candidates would have to pay more attention to building alliances with party leaders, in addition to at-

tempting to win support with the public. If the nomination decision is usually made only on the basis of popular appeal, a very extensive change in candidate behavior might result. For those who did engage in an active campaign, they would have to be much less concerned with winning pluralities and much more concerned with how they were being perceived by supporters of other candidates as a second- or third-choice preference. The importance of the active campaign itself might diminish considerably, as candidates would find little to gain by attempting to win committed delegates. If outsiders were blocked, those wishing to become candidates would have to channel their ambitions in an entirely different direction—toward establishing a reputation and a record of reliability in the years prior to the campaign, not during the campaign itself.

4. *Political Choice.*   The natural tendency, judging from the character of parties in the past, would be for a representative process to produce moderate candidates. However, much would depend on the particular plan adopted and on the evolving character of our party organizations, which cannot be known for certain. Because of the parties' tendency to produce moderate candidates, the whole question of choice should be viewed not simply in the framework of the nominating process of the major parties but in the framework of the electoral process as a whole. Receptivity to new ideas—to the extent they have support—can come from third parties, as has been the case in the past. Accordingly, an electoral system reasonably open to third parties, without doing anything to encourage them, might be an indirect part of any proposal for a representative decisionmaking process. The victories on ballot access won by John Anderson in 1980 can, from this perspective, be judged as in the long-range interest of the major parties.

At the same time, a representative process probably would work to discourage the kind of independent candidacy spawned by Anderson in 1980. The reason is more "psychological" than purely structural. Part of the difficulty with the current system is simply that it locks up the nomination far too early, giving some impetus to certain candidates and to the media to present the public with *new* alternatives. Merely maintaining the uncertainty and mystery of the nominations until a later point, which a representative process would do, would foreclose this source of third-party challenges. On the other hand, genuine third-party challenges, rooted in differences of program or philosophy, would remain unaffected.

5. *Effects on Governing.* A representative process, its proponents claim, would begin to rebuild parties and in so doing create a firmer tissue connecting the presidential candidate with members of his party in Congress and with other elected party members in the states. A presidential candidate's experience, as learned from the campaign, would teach him that power is not won and maintained merely by public opinion leadership, but also by forging connections with other officials in a political party. While the changes might not be dramatic, as many other factors besides the nominating process affect the character of presidential leadership, we might see a tendency for presidents to adopt a less "popular" style of leadership in favor of a more consultative style. What presidents might nominally lose in terms of discretion, they might gain in terms of effective power, for the day-to-day tasks of governing are more directly constrained by other officeholders than by marginal changes in public opinion.

6 AMERICAN PARTIES IN THE 1980s: Declining or Resurging?*

An unexpected and rather astonishing change seems to have occurred in the American political system since the 1980 election. Our political parties, diagnosed by most analysts as moribund before the election, did not expire; and while the Democratic party is still struggling, the Republican party appears more healthy and vigorous than at any other time in recent memory.

Yet whether there has been a real recovery of the institutional strength of political parties or merely a reshuffling of partisan forces remains unclear. Before reaching any hasty conclusions, it is important to examine the changing perceptions of party strength among political observers over the past few years. Prior to the 1980 election, analysts of American politics frequently spoke of a "decline" of American parties, a "decline" that was almost invariably thought irreversible. One of the most widely read books examining this issue—William Crotty and Gary C. Jacobson's *American Parties in Decline*,[1] published in 1980—took the commonly held position that the decline of parties was evident in virtually every area by which party strength is measured: in the loss of influence of party organizations in the nominations of presidential candidates, in the diminishing percentages of citizens identifying themselves as party ad-

*This chapter is a revised version of a lecture the author gave at Sangamon State University in March 1981 and wrote for the Centre D'Analyse Politique Comparée.

155

herents, in the declining impact of presidential election voting in congressional contests, and in the inability of parties to function effectively as instruments for coordinating policymaking between the president and the Congress.

As further evidence of party decline, analysts could point to early developments in the 1980 campaign, when for a moment it appeared that nomination by a major party, a prerequisite for election to the presidency since 1828, might no longer be necessary. A little-known congressman from Illinois, John Anderson, challenged the entire system of political parties by simply nominating himself as an "independent" candidate, a strategy he believed fit the nonpartisan tenor of the times. Anderson rose remarkably in the polls from a virtual unknown early in 1980 to the choice of 26 percent of the American electorate in June.[2] Was this, many wondered, a harbinger of a new era in American electoral politics?

The belief in the imminent decline of parties was quickly shaken, however, by the landslide presidential victory for Ronald Reagan and the impressive gains for the Republican party of thirty-three seats in the House and twelve seats in the Senate. The Senate victory, in fact, represented the largest number of seats that Republicans had ever gained at the expense of the Democrats. It was not just the size of the Republican victory, however, that impressed most observers; it was the *way* in which Republicans conducted the 1980 campaign. In recent American politics, candidates for Congress and the presidency have tended to run as individuals, de-emphasizing their party connection. But in 1980, most Republicans ran *as Republicans*, stressing their party affiliation and asking voters to change the *party* that held power in Washington; and since the inauguration of President Reagan—admittedly not a very long time—the Republicans in Congress have worked together quite well and have shown a surprising willingness to follow the lead of their president. Both Republicans and Democrats alike now seem to be operating on the assumption that the future of the Republican party, and for that matter the future of the Democratic party as well, rests with how the American people judge the success of the Republican economic program.

This apparent reversal in the strength of American parties has left many students of American politics puzzled, if not extremely embarrassed. When all is said and done, however, the questions about party strength remain unanswered. Were our political parties stronger before the 1980 election than most analysts claimed? Or are they weaker today than is generally believed? Or, finally, have the analysts been correct all along—that is, were the parties in fact declining in strength before the 1980 election and have they miraculously managed to revive themselves since?

As tempting as it might be to deal with the issue in terms of one of these alternatives, none of them, unfortunately, can adequately account for the recent developments in the party system. What confronts us in the entire debate over the question of party decline is a conceptual problem that requires a more careful definition of terms and an analysis of the causes of party strength. Only then can the current status of parties be addressed in a way that can make sense of recent developments.

This analysis is also needed to help sort out the potential impact of the apparent revival of parties on the debate over changing the presidential nominating process, for the two issues are closely linked. The fact of party revival (if true) seems to cut in two antithetical directions, both against and for institutional change. On the one hand, for advocates of measures to strengthen the parties, it raises certain questions about whether the previous circumstance of party weakness was as dire as many had thought, and it makes one wonder about the need for structural changes if, as seems the case today, parties are able to act so effectively under current arrangements. On the other hand, a revival of parties gives much comfort to advocates of change. For the past few years, many opponents of measures to strengthen parties have claimed that any such enterprise was futile and that the fate of parties was already doomed by forces beyond the control of party leaders and legislators. Now, however, that there are signs of self-regeneration in our party system, these defeatist objections seem particularly inappropriate. Only as we begin to understand the sense in which parties may be revived is it possible to weigh the respective merits of these two arguments.

THE CAUSES OF PARTY STRENGTH

From an analytic standpoint, four basic causes underlie the strengths (or weaknesses) of our political parties. The first is the prevailing attitude or doctrine toward political parties—that is, the dominant opinion, held either by elites or the public, about the role that parties should play in the American political system. All institutions vary in strength and character according to what people think their functions should be. For example, the widespread belief in a limited presidency that grew up during the Jefferson era was one factor that helped restrict the growth of executive power in the nineteenth century, just as the belief in a powerful presidency that emerged with Teddy Roosevelt and Woodrow Wilson helped to pave the way for the emergence of the dynamic, twentieth-century chief executive. The doctrinal cause of institutional strength is especially important in the case of political parties because unlike the presidency and Congress parties have in the Constitution no status that provides them with a fixed base of authority. Their strength is therefore more readily influenced by what people think their role should be, and in this sense, parties are the most malleable of all our national institutions.

To understand more clearly the nature of the doctrinal explanation of party strength, it will be helpful to cite an example of a contemporary scholar who has made use of this cause to account for developments in the party system during the last decade. Austin Ranney recently offered the following observation on Americans' attitude toward the major parties:

> Americans . . . deal uneasily with the necessities of partisan political organization because of their widespread belief that political parties are, at best, unavoidable evils whose propensities for divisiveness, oligarchy and corruption must be closely watched and sternly controlled.[3]

Ranney went on to explore elite opinions toward parties, noting the growth of the reform view that favored the regulation of parties and that fit very nicely with the generally suspicious attitude toward parties held by the general public.

The second cause of party strength derives from legal and structural factors, meaning party rules and federal and state law, including Court decisions, that bear directly on the powers and arrangement of the parties. Legal and structural factors are often linked closely to doctrines about parties, for the obvious reason that legislators and party officials usually write laws and rules to reflect their conception of the role that parties should play. Because of this connection, it is often possible to speak of these two causes at the same time without distinguishing between them. Yet the two causes are different and frequently operate in tension with each other. These differences result, among other reasons, from legal changes that are adopted, without regard to doctrines about parties, by institutions like the

Court or state legislatures, whose priorities may be different; and from laws and rules that have consequences other than—even contrary to—those originally intended by legislators.

As an example of a legal (and doctrinal) explanation of party strength, one can cite a passage from a recent essay by Jean Kirkpatrick:

> ... the most important sources of party decomposition are the *decisions* taken by persons attempting to reform the parties. Some of these efforts at party reform have aimed to weaken one or both parties ... others [were] undertaken to perfect the political process but have had the unintended effect of hastening party deinstitutionalization. ... Of all of [the] reasons for the continuing decline in the parties' ability to perform their traditional functions, I have stressed reform. Whether undertaken by the parties, the Congress, or the courts, reform, along with its intended and unintended consequences, is, I believe, the most important cause of this decline.[4]

The third cause of party strength derives from what, for want of a better term, can be called environmental factors, that is, developments affecting parties that arise from changes in social structure or in the state of communications technology. This category includes the rise of the so-called new class in modern postindustrial societies and the vast changes in electioneering that have resulted from the advent of television, campaign polling, and the use of computers.

Many contemporary scholars have relied on environmental factors to explain the strength of our parties. Everett C. Ladd, Jr., for example, thinks the impact of the new class and the associated rise in educational levels account, in great part, for the decline in parties:

> A large segment of the [American] electorate now describes itself as independent. ... Higher levels of information bearing on political issues and hence a higher measure of issue orientation, and a general feeling of confidence in one's ability to judge candidates and their programs apart from party links, are promoted by the experience of higher education. ... An electorate which is highly educated ... will be bound less by partisan identification in its electoral behavior. This cause of party irregularity is unlikely to recede.[5]

Arthur Schlesinger, Jr., the famous historian, stresses the communications revolution:

> Some political scientists blame the decline of parties on the reform movement of the last decade. But party reform was a response, not a cause. ... The reason for the deep and perhaps incurable crisis of the system lies ... above all

in the organic change wrought in the political environment by the electronic revolution.[6]

The fourth and final cause of party strength derives from the prevailing political context, meaning the importance of issues confronting the nation at any particular time, the way in which statesmen present these issues, and the degree to which party members share a common public philosophy and act together as participants in a genuine association having a political purpose. Scholars of critical realignments in American electoral history have emphasized this idea of a periodic surge and decline of partisan commitment. At certain moments, when the political climate is charged with heated debate over profound issues, members of one or both of the parties (or perhaps a third party) become firm advocates of a political cause; at other moments, when the issues presented are of less perceptible importance, one finds less commitment and enthusiasm, and members may remain with their party more from habit or interest than from principle.

Alexis de Tocqueville was the first analyst of American politics to identify the significance of the political context for influencing the character and strength of political parties. In making his classic distinction between "great parties" and "small parties," Tocqueville observed:

> There are times when nations are tormented by such great ills that the idea of a total change in their political constitution comes into mind. . . . That is the time of . . . great parties. . . . There are times when the human spirit believes itself firmly settled on certain fundamentals and does not seek to look beyond a fixed horizon. That is a time for . . . small parties. . . . Great political parties are those more attached to principles than to consequences [while] . . . small parties are generally without political faith.[7]

Modern realignment theorists have adapted this distinction to fit the milder pulse of conflict within American history. As James Sundquist has written:

> When a community goes through a realignment period, it is in the grip of an issue of transcendent power. The voters who have polarized on the issue have experienced deep emotions . . . these emotions are transferred to the parties. [After a crisis] the parties lose the sense of moral purpose that energized them in the crisis. They become cautious. Participation in party affairs slackens. . . . People are again heard to say "The parties don't stand for anything" and "there's no difference between the parties."[8]

THE CHARACTERISTICS OF THE FOUR CAUSES

These four causes of party strength—the doctrinal, the legal, the environmental, and the political—are *analytic* categories; in the real world, they are clearly not isolated or fully independent causes, but rather—as is ordinarily the case with causes in the social sciences—interact with each other in a complex cause-and-effect relationship. To make sense of our world, however, simplification is necessary, and these causes therefore will be treated initially as discrete variables.

Each cause has certain general properties or characteristics. Doctrinal and legal factors, which can be discussed together, tend to exert a steady influence over a long period of time. Prevailing consensuses about the role of parties and basic legal configurations do not change very often. Over the course of American history, there have been only five identifiable "systems" of presidential nomination (see Chapters 2 and 3), which is the most important function performed by the national parties. Each of these systems was characterized by a rough correspondence between doctrinal and legal factors, a correspondence that was usually upset just before a new system replaced its predecessor.

Although doctrines and basic structural configurations do not change very often, they *can* be changed through deliberate and conscious intervention. Opinion leaders and legislators are in a position to influence attitudes toward parties, and party officials and legislators have the legal authority to change party structures.[9] Political scientists tend to focus a great deal of attention on legal structures, not because they are the only or even necessarily the most important cause of the strength and character of an institution, but because they constitute the element over which political actors have the most control. Through their authority to devise rules and pass laws, party leaders and legislators can attempt to build a party structure that will exert certain influences for a relatively long period of time. Of course, these legal structures may only be able to promote their intended results if certain environmental factors prevail, and intelligent legislative efforts must therefore attempt to take into account the way in which legal factors interact with their environment.

The third cause that influences party strength, environmental factors, also produces long-term effects. Although environmental influences can change unexpectedly in response to new socioeconomic and technological developments, for the most part basic environmental influences such as the class structure or the prevailing communications system endure for an entire era. They are "constants" that continually shape the operation of the political system.

Unlike doctrinal and legal causes, environmental factors are largely beyond the control of political actors. This does not mean that legislators are unable to regulate certain aspects of their influence. In France, for example, election polls cannot be published the week prior to the election in an effort to limit the impact of this technological development on election results.[10] Yet such legislative measures, although not insignificant, remain limited in their impact on the influences exerted by basic environmental factors. Ultimately, these influences are beyond legislative control, especially in free societies. Legislators cannot fully control basic socioeconomic forces, nor can they do more than adjust the context within which technological change influences political life.

The fourth cause of party strength, the political context, is characterized by the absence of any qualitative change, in the sense that there is no end to the general pattern of variation in intensity of political action. Although August Comte and Karl Marx predicted an "end" to politics, an end that might conceivably come at some point in the future, for now it is safe to say that as long as we have politics, we will have episodic surges and declines in the intensity with which people view political affairs.

The political context, accordingly, presents the nation and its party system with an ever-changing series of stimuli. At certain moments, as already observed, issues are perceived as more important than usual, and people come together either in new parties or under the umbrella of an existing party label and form genuine associations committed to pursuing a common public philosophy. When the intensity of commitment is especially strong, a party will probably find some way to work temporarily in unison, even if the legal arrangement under which the party operates works against strong parties. At other moments, when the intensity is absent or when the party members share no common public philosophy, effective coordination—at least in the American system of separated powers—may be difficult to achieve, even where legal factors promote strong parties by American standards.

The fact that politics is characterized by ceaseless variation in the intensity of issue concern should not be construed to mean that the driving force behind issues derives from factors that are always beyond rational human control. While new agendas are often generated by new circumstances of the economy and the social structure, they are also often the result of deliberate and conscious efforts by political thinkers and statesmen to bring about change. Ideas continually generate new problems and issues for politics, and it is precisely because people disagree on the plane of theoretical conceptions of politics that political debate and change never cease. Indeed, in democratic societies, it is *not* the purpose of institutional arrangements to attempt to end political controversy, but to create a setting in which controversies are moderated and settled in ways that do not destroy the society.

A DEFINITION OF PARTY STRENGTH AND THE CURRENT STATUS OF AMERICAN PARTIES

Keeping this analysis of the causes of party strength in mind, it is time to return to the question of what it means to say that American political parties have undergone a change in strength. A change could refer conceivably to a strengthening or weakening of parties that results from any one of these four factors. Yet most analysts, when they speak of a change, probably have in mind not a temporary cyclical downturn or upturn, but rather a long-term trend that results in stronger or weaker parties across entire cycles of political variation. Party strength, in other words, normally should be understood as a function of long-term institutional properties, meaning the influences exerted by doctrinal, legal, and environmental causes, *not* political causes. To the extent that parties change in strength because of the political context, it is important to stipulate that this *is* the reason.

During the 1970s, when political analysts began to remark on the phenomenon of party decline, it was especially difficult to distinguish among these four causes because all of them were impelling parties in the same direction. Parties grew weaker because of the doctrinal attack of reform; because of the adoption of party rules and laws that, intentionally or inadvertently, took powers and functions away from the party organizations; because of socioeconomic and technological changes that made it more difficult for parties to operate effectively; and finally because the dominant party of the era, the Democratic party, lost its sense of public purpose and had no program or approach for dealing with the issues of the day. Indeed, because all of these causes were leading toward the same result, some analysts failed to keep clear in their own minds the different sources of the change; everything was lumped together into a single, undifferentiated phenomenon—the decline of parties—which was used frequently as an explanatory factor in its own right, independent of the factors that caused it.

If the different causes of party strength are kept in mind, however, formulating a comprehensive interpretation of what has happened to American parties in the past decade should be possible. Their status can be summarized and analyzed by examining four theses: (1) Political parties have become weaker over the past decade, and this condition has changed only marginally in the last year; (2) the weakness of American parties before the 1980 election was exaggerated because of the failure to recognize the short-term impact of political factors; (3) the strength of the parties today is also likely to be exaggerated, and political factors are contributing temporarily to the strength of the Republican party; and (4) the situation today presents a new opportunity for genuine party revitalization through structural changes.

Thesis I

Political parties have become much weaker since 1968. In the very recent past (1979–81), this condition has changed only marginally, with some factors leading to further decline and others promoting a slight strengthening.

The visible and measurable indices of party decline, such as partisan identification and party-line voting in Congress, have already been mentioned.[11] Of greater interest are the broad consequences of party decline on the operation of the American political system. Defenders of strong political parties from Martin Van Buren in the nineteenth century to contemporary political scientists like Nelson Polsby have argued their case on the grounds that effective parties perform certain beneficial functions. Parties serve as mechanisms for building and maintaining relatively broad and stable coalitions; they channel and moderate the ambitions of presidential aspirants by "forcing" candidates to become consensual leaders; they discipline factions and interest groups by making them partake in the give and take of coalitional politics; and they provide a supplementary extra-constitutional instrument for facilitating cooperation between the president and Congress in a separation-of-powers system.

Accordingly, a system of party competition dominated by two relatively strong parties can be viewed as a political institution that promotes certain tendencies and patterns of behavior. As parties decline and no similar structures take their place, a process of de-institutionalization occurs—a situation in which there are fewer (or no) specifiable tendencies or patterns of behavior. The result of de-institutionalization is disaggregation and volatility, conditions in which political activity moves now one way and now another in response to short-term and contingent factors. This kind of volatile politics has become more characteristic of American politics as parties have grown weaker.

The effects of the recent de-institutionalization of the party system have been most evident in the presidential selection system (see Chapter 3). Within Congress, the modestly centralizing role that parties once played has also decreased during the last decade, at least up to the time that President Reagan came to power. Of course, in the 1960s, parties were already rather weak instruments: one must go all the way back to the period of Speaker Joseph G. Cannon at the turn of this century to find truly powerful congressional parties. By its nature as a representative system with independent local constituencies, the American political system does not promote party government in Congress. Nevertheless, before the 1970s presidents and congressional party leaders could at least attempt to forge a consensus by forming alliances among a few highly powerful committee chairmen. The reforms in Congress in the 1970s, especially in the House, served to decentralize authority from the committees to the subcommittees—which number some 139 in the House alone. Under these circumstances coordination has become more difficult, and congressional policymaking behavior has been schizophrenic, alternating between sluggishness (as in energy legislation) and stampede (as in environmental legislation early in the 1970s.[12] In a de-institutionalized setting, these unpredictable and dramatically different results are exactly what one might expect. The success of the Republican party in holding ranks after the 1980 election, it is clear, has been based not on any structural changes—there have been none—but on (temporary) political factors that have cemented the party together.

Finally, national campaign finance legislation passed in the 1970s has moved control of funding even further from the parties and has stimulated the activity of Political Action Committees (PACs), which, in effect, are rivals to political parties. Indeed, in this area, it can be said that rather than seeing a process of de-institutionalization we are witnessing the beginning of an institutionalized system that works to the detriment of political parties. Again, as in the case of parties in Congress a decade ago, parties in the 1960s were *not* very influential sources of fundraising. Most funds for political campaigns were raised by the individual candidates for office, with the largest contributions coming from individual citizens. The campaign finance legislation put limits on the contributions of individuals and groups, as well as providing public funding for presidential campaigns, but it has evolved in such a way that groups have distinct advantages. Political Action Committees can give more money to campaigns than can individuals ($5,000 per campaign for groups compared to $1,000 for individuals). Much more important, the law allows independent expenditures for campaigns without limit as long as the money spent is not coordinated directly by the candidates' official campaign organization. While both individuals and groups can make these expenditures, in practice PACs have spent most of the independent money, since they possess the organization and political sophistication to mount campaign activities. The law therefore has created an incentive for the formation of these groups, and in recent years, there has been a tremendous increase in both their number and activity. Many of these groups promote specialized interests or ideological viewpoints, and the campaign finance legislation has therefore served to increase the influence of factional groups at the expense of the moderating effect of political parties.

Since the late 1970s, changes in party structure have only marginally affected the strength of American parties. Confirming the trend of structural decline, presidential nominees were again chosen by a de facto system of direct democracy, with the national Democratic Convention even going so far as to adopt a rule allowing national candidates to replace delegates who threatened to break their pledges. In addition, in the 1978 and 1980 congressional campaigns and in the 1980 presidential campaign, independent expenditures by PACs rose dramatically.

There were, however, two changes that promoted the strength of parties. In the Republican party, the national chairman, William Brock, undertook a remarkable effort to enhance the capacities of the national organization and succeeded in substantially augmenting the assistance, both financial and technical, that the national party provided congressional candidates, state parties, and even candidates for state office. The budget of the Republican National Committee rose from $6.5 million in 1974 to $17.5 million in 1979, and the organizational groundwork laid by the party for the 1980 election was the envy of the Democrats. Democrats are now trying to emulate the Republican effort, and it appears that stronger national staffs are likely to become a permanent part of American party organization. Both of the new party chairmen, Richard Richards for the GOP and Charles Manatt for the Democrats, are committed to building stronger parties.

The second change, seemingly very technical, nonetheless had a significant impact on party organizational activity in the 1980 presidential campaign. Under the campaign finance legislation passed in 1976, the amount of money that state and local organizations could raise and spend on behalf of their presidential nominee was limited, which depressed participation in local organizational activities. In 1979, an amendment to the campaign finance legislation lifted most of these restrictions and permitted the state and local parties to spend as much as they could raise for certain campaign activities, including voter registration, volunteer assistance, and efforts to bring voters to the polls. This change enabled the Republican state and local parties to spend $15 million on behalf of Ronald Reagan. (The Democrats spent only $5 million.) More important than the sums spent was the increase in citizen involvement in party affairs; and from a theoretical (and practical) perspective, the law demonstrated the significance of legal factors in affecting party strength.

Thesis II

The weakness of parties before the 1980 election, however, was frequently exaggerated. Political factors contributing in the short term to the decline of parties were not always carefully identified, with the result that many overstated the extent of the decline and underestimated the potential of parties to serve as vehicles for political realignments.

Although the decline of parties as institutions over the last decade has been significant, the extent of this decline was probably exaggerated before the 1980 election. The political context, with its cyclical "ups" and "downs," worked in the last decade to depress still further the effectiveness of the parties. Specifically, the Democratic party, which had been the majority party in America ever since the election of Roosevelt in 1932, lost a clear sense of unity and purpose, which was symbolized during the 1976 campaign by the failure of the leading presidential aspirants to characterize themselves as "liberals." Franklin Roosevelt introduced the term "liberalism" into American politics in the 1930s to describe the Democratic party's public philosophy of the positive or welfare state, and thereafter, liberalism had served as the core defining the party's program. By the 1970s, however, many Democratic politicians either rejected liberalism or chose not to identify openly with that label. Indeed, the last Democratic president, Jimmy Carter, was anything but a liberal in the classic American sense.

The extent of the Democrats' loss of a common public philosophy can best be appreciated by contrasting the performance of the Democratic party from 1976 to 1980 with the high expectations that many had for the party just after the 1976 election. James Sundquist, one of America's most astute electoral analysts, argued in an article in 1976 that the Democratic party was now prepared to assume control and provide a coordinated program. Sundquist based his argument in part on the contention that the old southern wing of the party, which had been preoccupied with stopping the civil rights revolution, was now dead. With southern Democrats now more like their northern and western colleagues, there would be no impediment to the Democrats' enacting their liberal programs. In Sundquist's words:

> On the Democratic side, the old anti–New Deal "bourbon" wing that thwarted and frustrated Democratic presidents from Franklin Roosevelt to John Kennedy has been dwindling rapidly.... There is at least solid reason to believe that the prospect for an effective, lasting partnership between the president and Congress has never been better than it will be during the era that the inauguration of President Carter has ushered in. The long season of hostility and stalemate between the branches should have passed. The American government should begin to work again.[13]

Sundquist would certainly be the first to admit that this cooperation among Democrats failed to materialize during the Carter administration. This failure did not result from the opposition of "bourbon" southern Democrats—Sundquist was correct on this point—but from the fact that the entire party had lost its sense of direction. Most of the old conservatives were gone, but the "new" party was not committed to a liberal program—indeed, it was no longer certain what liberalism meant—and in the first year of the Reagan administration, many southern Democrats in Congress, although not "bourbons" of the old school, nevertheless found the conservatism of the Republican party more to their liking than the positions taken by their own Democratic leadership. This alliance between Republicans and southern Democrats in the House gave President Reagan his stunning successes on the budget and tax votes in the spring and summer of 1981.

The decline of liberalism is clearly too large and complex a topic to discuss here in any detail. It is worth noting the general point, however, that liberalism suffered a decline in part because of its success. By the end of the 1960s, liberals had completed action on many of their most important programs for social welfare and civil rights. Their search for new issues and a new agenda helped split the party and alienate many traditional party adherents. The new agenda consisted on the one hand of programs to enforce greater equality, including the busing of schoolchildren to achieve racial balance, affirmative action and quotas for minorities, and schemes for income redistribution. On the other hand, it consisted of liberalism on "social" and cultural issues, including advocacy of more freedom of expression, more protection for the rights of the accused and criminals, women's rights, the right to abortion, and environmentalism. On these social issues, American public opinion was highly divided, and many former liberals rejected the "new" liberalism.

Finally, in the late 1970s, the American people began to believe that liberalism, understood as big government, was not working. Whereas from the period of the New Deal until the 1970s, the expansion of the welfare state seemed compatible with a healthy and growing economy, by the mid-1970s this no longer appeared to be the case. During the 1970s, the American economy entered a period of low growth, high inflation, high unemployment, and increasing taxes. Whether or not the growing size of the public sector and the large deficits were the main causes for these economic problems—a question on which economists themselves disagreed—the public increasingly came to *think* that big government was the problem. Between

1976 and 1980, the Democratic party either bore the responsibility for this economic situation or had the misfortune of controlling the government as conditions deteriorated. During the 1980 election, a Gallup poll showed that voters felt that Ronald Reagan was likely to do a better job on every major economic issue, including not only controlling inflation and dealing with the energy problem but also reducing unemployment, a traditional Democratic party strong point.[14] The public philosophy of liberalism was itself divided and confused about how to deal with the economic situation, alternately preaching forbearance with lowered expectations and bold new controls of the economy by public authorities.

It was, accordingly, ideological disarray—and not just the structural weakness of parties—that accounted for much of the disaggregation in the Democratic party and its inability to hold together and govern effectively during the years of the Carter administration. And to this, one must add the special political factor of a congressional wing of the party that had lost the discipline that comes from the threat of being unseated: the Democratic party control of both Houses of Congress from 1956 to 1980 was the longest for any party since permanent party competition began in the 1820s.

During the 1970s, Republicans were unable to articulate clearly an alternative public philosophy, or at any rate were unable to convince Americans of the viability of their programs. The Watergate affair also damaged any hope of a Republican resurgence. Thus, while one party was down, the other was not up. The political situation was characterized by the ideological disarray of the majority party and the seeming weakness of the minority party. American politics was in a strange interlude.

Many electoral analysts, among them Walter Dean Burnham, saw this interlude as yet another manifestation of the general decline of political parties.[15] Although the political circumstances peculiar to the decade may have contributed to the disarray, these analysts argued that the chief reason for America's inability to recover from this malaise lay with the weakness of our political parties. Realignment, which had been the traditional means of regeneration and recovery, was unlikely or impossible in light of the debilitated condition of the parties.

This analysis, however, probably assumed too much. Its underlying premise seemed to be that the existence of the interlude in the 1970s was a unique phenomenon and therefore proof of the fact that parties had lost their capacity to serve as vehicles for realignments.

Even if this reading of history was correct, however, it would not prove the point of party incapacity today. Merely because events have occurred in a certain way in three instances in the past does not constitute a clear presumption that the pattern must repeat itself. All historical analogies should leave room for special and contingent factors such as the effect of an abnormal crisis like Watergate. In point of fact, moreover, the historical record does not support the claim that the disarray of the 1970s was unique. Prior to the realigning election of 1896, for example, there had been a rather long period in which the majority party (the Republicans) lost a clear sense of purpose and began to decline, but in which the Democrats had been unable to gain the upper hand. Periods of political disaggregation may be natural preludes to periods of renewal.

The view that parties were incapable of shouldering the burden of a realignment failed to give sufficient weight to the importance of the political context as a cause of political disaggregation in the 1870s. Although parties clearly grew weaker as institutions after 1968, the cause of the interlude of the 1970s may have been just as much the result of political factors—that is, of the absence of agreement on any common purpose in the majority party—as it was the result of the structural decline of the parties.

It would be foolish, of course, to go to the opposite extreme and claim that party structure is irrelevant to the entire process of re-alignment. A more reasonable hypothesis would appear to be that parties that are weak structurally but strong in their commitment to a common purpose remain capable of initiating a realignment; however, a new majority party that lacks strength as an institution may find it difficult or impossible to gather the energy and maintain the consistency needed to *sustain* a majority and carry out its program for an entire era.

Thesis III

The strength of our parties in 1981 (such as it is now sometimes perceived) also may be exaggerated. Just as political factors contributed to the weakness of parties during the last decade, so they may be contributing "artificially" to their strength today, temporarily masking their real weaknesses.

The discussion of this thesis is the obverse of the second thesis. In 1980, the Republican party emerged as a genuine association of individuals committed to a basic public philosophy. Despite all the structural factors that make for weak parties in America, the strength of this common commitment has served to forge a unity among Republicans and has transformed the party into a formidable policymaking instrument. Indeed, if the Republican party controlled the House of Representatives today, one probably would have seen decisive, coordinated action of the kind that occurred after the elections of 1932 and 1964; and even with the House in Democratic hands, President Reagan has demonstrated enough support in the nation to pressure many Democrats, especially from the South, to back important aspects of his program. Weak party structures in the Congress paradoxically worked to the president's advantage, enabling him to secure needed support from the opposition party.

Of course, the Republican party today is not completely unified in every respect. American parties seldom, if ever, achieve total unity. There are currently three basic domains of Republican policy: (1) The economic program consisting of a plan to reduce the growth of the domestic public sector by program cuts and to stimulate private incentives through cuts in the marginal tax rate; (2) the foreign policy program, consisting of a plan to increase significantly America's military strength and to rekindle the suspicions of Americans toward communism and the Soviet Union; and (3) the "social" policy program, consisting of opposition to the Equal Rights Amendment, pledges to end federal support for abortion, and proposals to stimulate private and religious schools as alternatives to public education.

Republicans are united on the first part of their economic program, which calls for cuts in the size of the domestic budget, but there is some disagreement on "supply side" theories that would cut taxes and leave substantial budget deficits for at least the next four years. Republicans are also united on a basic foreign policy program, although its tenets are so general that they leave much room for disagreement on particular measures. On social issues, however, the Republican party enjoys at most a nominal unity. Most Republicans generally take a more "conservative" posture than Democrats on these issues; yet the party clearly is divided between moderates on the one side and elements of the "New Right" and the "Moral Majority" on the other. The former are content to maintain the status quo on social issues or to proceed very cautiously, while the latter are pressing for quick action on a whole range of social issues.

These disagreements among Republicans are significant. But until the most controversial aspects of these social issues come up for consideration, Republicans should be able to maintain a broadly unified front. Their differences are less significant than their common opposition to liberal programs; and as long as liberalism remains a possible alternative, Republicans will have the incentive to settle their differences through bargain and compromise. Thus, at present the centripetal forces tending to unite the Republican party are stronger than the centrifugal forces leading to disintegration.

For Republicans, however, the challenge is not merely whether they can remain united but also whether they can win the support of a majority of the electorate (see Table 6-1). For an entire generation, public opinion polls have shown the Republican party to be the minority party in regard to partisan preference, and even the election of 1980 did not change this result. The Democratic party clearly continues to maintain a potential majority base of support among American voters.

Yet there are strong reasons for supposing that these figures do not accurately describe the actual condition of the American electorate. Party identification is no longer as accurate a predictor of actual voting behavior as it once was, and many who still claim a Democratic preference actually vote Republican fairly regularly. Moreover, the growth of independents may also indicate a loosening of the grip of Democrats on their following and the beginning of a possible trend toward the Republican party. Indeed, because partisan preference polls have never before been taken during a realigning period, social scientists have no way of knowing how partisan preferences actually would change in the initial stages of a realignment. A reasonable hypothesis, however, is that a change in voting behavior would precede the formal declaration of a change in party preference. Analysis of the election results and a common-sense weighing of ideological and electoral trends therefore may constitute a better

Table 6-1. Party Identification in America, 1960-80.

	1960	1964	1968	1972	1976	1980
Democrats	47%	53%	46%	42%	48%	32%
Independents	23	22	27	31	29	41
Republicans	30	25	27	27	23	25

Source: 1960-76, Gallup Polls; 1980 (postelection), ABC-Washington Post Sunday (March 1, 1981).

method of assessing the possibilities of realignment than a narrow, but detailed, analysis of partisan preference polls.

As a phenomenon of mass politics in America, a realignment can be defined as a fundamental shift in public opinion about the role of government in society and the ends or objectives of the political system as a whole. Thus, the change that occurred in the 1930s, from support of the limited or negative state to support of the positive or welfare state, represented a realignment. Realignments are usually, although not always, associated with major changes in the partisan orientation of the voters, since political parties generally serve as the vehicles for either initiating or ratifying the proposed change in public philosophy. The party that manages successfully to initiate or identify itself with the dominant new public philosophy becomes the majority party of the ensuing era. The minority party, of course, will win some elections in the interim, but its victories are attributable to special, short-term factors, such as nominating an extremely popular candidate (for instance, Dwight D. Eisenhower) or capitalizing on the temporary failures of the majority party (as the Republicans did in the cases of the Korean and Vietnam wars).

Realignments are more, however, than changes in public opinion or partisan voting patterns. They are also one of the mechanisms in American politics that supply the energy and political power to accomplish fundamental changes in policy. They constitute, so to speak, America's "mini-revolutions." By establishing the basic political configurations for an entire era, realignments enable major political leaders, like President Lincoln and President Roosevelt, to influence the political context in the nation long after they have left office. No president having in mind a dramatic shift in the nation's politics can hope to accomplish all his goals in the course of one or even two terms. To fix indelibly his imprint on American public life, a president must find a way to retain influence even after he has left office. Realignment is such a means. It allows a president to articulate a new majority public philosophy that sets the terms of the debate for future policymaking; and it bequeaths to the president's successors the political support—in the form of the majority party status—that can accomplish the long process of turning out the laws, rules, and myriad bureaucratic decisions that transform a set of ideas into public policy.

If the condition of American politics is analyzed according to this definition of realignments, it would appear that America is in the midst of a realignment that may or may not be completed. Realignments involve a change in public opinion from one public philosophy to another, and today the American public has gone through only half of that process. The American people have rejected, at least for the time being, the old liberal public philosophy of an expanding welfare state; but the American people have not yet adopted the new public philosophy of Ronald Reagan's conservatism. The accomplishment of the Republican campaign of 1980 was impressive but limited: It did not convert the American people to conservatism, but it did convince a majority of the voters, in circumstances short of an outright crisis, that conservatism was credible enough to deserve a *chance* to work its proposed solutions.

Predicting realignments from election results alone is in any case a fruitless endeavor because realignments in the final analysis are forged not in elections but in the process of governing. The conditions for a realignment today are clearly present: President Reagan now has set forth a relatively coherent domestic program that contrasts starkly with the direction of politics in the period of Democratic dominance and that embodies a new public philosophy respecting the role of government in American society. The realignment the president seeks, however, will stand a chance of being completed only if by 1984 his economic program shows tangible signs of success as measured by the rate of inflation and the growth of the economy. Even then, to ensure that the new public philosophy can be sustained over an entire era and supported by a firm majority, future Republican presidents will need the backing of a stronger party structure.

The Republican party today is held together by the euphoria of its recent victory and its momentary enthusiasm and commitment to a broad political program. It is sailing on a summer sea. When the flush of victory and newly won power begin to fade, however, and when more difficult times arrive, as they inevitably will, the unity of the Republican party may quickly dissipate. The Republican party is not nearly so strong as it appears today.

For a party to sustain its support for a general program for an entire era, it needs a cadre of organizational regulars who subscribe to a common set of beliefs and who maintain a powerful position in the nomination of the party's presidential candidates. The nomination of presidential candidates by direct democracy ultimately undermines this base of stability, thereby diminishing the likelihood that a party can maintain an ideological center of gravity. It is quite true that in recent times Democrats have experienced this problem of inconsistency more than Republicans; but this has been a natural result of the Republicans' smaller and more homogeneous base. With this more restricted base, the Republican party was able to function with less internal inconsistency even under a system of direct democracy, although the unity of the party was threatened by the split between moderates and conservatives in 1976.

Paradoxically, however, if the Republican party should manage to become the majority party in the years ahead, it may well face the same problems that the Democrats have had. The flow of large numbers of new adherents into the party, probably only partly committed to its principles, soon could weaken the party's sense of purpose and direction. These adherents, voting in Republican presidential primaries, might well allow the momentary struggles of the day to occupy the center ground in their decisions, leaving the Republican party as a label to be captured by one or another faction or candidate. Committed Republicans might soon find the title to their party disputed and then usurped, something they may wish to consider as their electoral position improves.

Thesis IV

The situation today presents a new opportunity for genuine party revitalization through structural changes. The doctrine of "reform" that contributed to the decline of parties has itself begun to decline. This change in the climate of opinion has increased the freedom of party officials and legislators to take conscious steps to strengthen the parties.

Party leaders and legislators concerned with the institutional strength of America's political parties find themselves today in a markedly different situation today than the one they were in before the 1980 election. Not only did the 1980 election demonstrate that large partisan swings in congressional representation, and even realignment, are still possible, but it also showed that the doctrinal support for direct democracy has collapsed, bringing the nation to the end of the era of reform. This collapse made it possible for the former Democratic party chairman, John White, to call for "corrections" of the reforms and for the recently appointed head of a new Democratic Commission, Governor James Hunt of North Carolina, to state:

> We are about the business of trying to elect a president, and we need to nominate and elect that person in such a way that that person can govern effectively.[16]

There is almost certainly a connection between this broad shift away from reform and the ideological movements discussed above. As Samuel Beer has shown in a perceptive essay on modern liberalism, the reform ethos of the last decade was itself an outgrowth of liberalism and perhaps an early sign of its exhaustion.[17] As liberals lost a sense of mission about *what* should be done, many in the party turned to a sterile preoccupation with *how* things should be done, convincing themselves for a time that the latter was a genuine substitute for the former. It is true, of course, that in the initial stages of reform there seemed to be some short-term links between substance and procedures, principally in the case of the Vietnam War, which many felt could be stopped by making the nominating process more democratic. By the mid-1970s, however, the connections between democratic procedures and substantive goals became less and less apparent; and while some liberals held firm to their commitment to further procedural reforms, others began to have second thoughts. By 1980, these thoughts were being expressed openly, thus helping to dampen the enthusiasm for direct democracy.

Whether party leaders and legislators will take advantage of their new freedom to act remains an open question. The Democrats, surprisingly, seem on the verge of leading the battle against the reforms. Although the movement for reform sprang initially from their own ranks, more and more Democrats have come to realize that it is their party that may have lost the most from the present system. The Republicans, who have suffered less from the reforms, may be slower to act. They are not, like the Democrats, at all used to the idea of national party commissions that legislate change. Then, too, there is in the modern conservative movement a powerful "populist" streak that differentiates it somewhat from the more restrained conservatism of the past. Many present-day conservatives, having profited from many of these populist devices, may therefore be reluctant to sacrifice certain momentary advantages for what are—or what used to be—conservative principles favoring representative decisionmaking methods. As Harvey Mansfield, a sympathetic observer of the current Republican party, has counseled:

> Reagan would be well advised to find his conservatism in the Constitution [and the principle of representation] rather than to adopt a conservative populism. If he does the latter, he is likely to discover that the radical means of populism will overcome and outlast the conservative ends.[18]

CONCLUSION

While a hasty reading of this chapter might lead one to think that institutional issues of party structure and nominating procedures are irrelevant, this clearly would be the wrong conclusion to draw. The point of the rather complex analysis that has been made is to place institutional factors in their proper perspective in relationship to political events, attributing to them neither more nor less influence than they merit.

In distinguishing among the various causes of party strength, it became clear that one cause—the political context—strongly influences the short-term strength of political parties irrespective of party structure. In those unusual instances in which individuals from a genuine association of common purpose adhere to a coherent public philosophy and win a firm majority, a strong party structure may be unnecessary for a party to act effectively in the short run. Such is the case today with the Republican party. In instances in which a party is made up of individuals who share no common public philosophy and who have lost a sense of common purpose, a strong party structure may be of little help. Such was the case for the Democratic party in the 1970s, and a strong party structure probably would not have saved the party completely.

These two instances, however, represent the extremes of the political situation. Most of the time, political activity takes place in circumstances between these extremes. It is then that the institutional structures of parties can make the critical marginal differences between a political system in which a modicum of effective coordination can be squeezed from a narrow consensus and a political system in which disaggregation and volatility are the order of the day.

7 CONCLUSION

Legislators of the nominating process today face a fundamental choice—whether to maintain the present system of direct democracy, with its limited role for political parties, or whether to transform the system into a representative decisionmaking process under the auspices of the political parties. In making this choice, legislators need to consider three general questions. Is a system based on discretionary representative decisionmaking preferable to the current system? Is it possible or feasible to institute such a system? And assuming an affirmative response to both of these questions, what would be the best strategy and plan for carrying out the needed changes?

PREFERENCE

In the favorite terms of its own defenders, the virtue of the current system is its "openness." Another way, perhaps, to describe this same quality is to say that the current system has de-institutionalized the nominating process, eliminating institutional forms that produced certain definite tendencies and substituting for them a highly unstructured (or "open") process that functions less predictably and responds more directly to current and contingent factors. This formulation may initially strike defenders of the current system as "loaded" and unfair, but in reality, it incorporates to a large extent the reformers' own assessment of the nominating problem. Progressives and recent reformers attacked existing representative nomination systems not because they were unstructured but precisely because they *were* structured to produce consequences that these proponents of change considered undesirable. Representative systems were said to be too "moderate" and to extract too high a price in corruption and in deference to traditional political groups. For their part, the defenders of representative systems, whether of the pure convention or the "mixed" variety, responded by pointing out the benefits of party decisionmaking and by attacking the formlessness and volatility that would accompany direct democracy. And so the debate raged during the Progressive era and again during the past decade.

These arguments between the opponents and the defenders of previous representative systems are not, however, fully applicable to the current debate. History never simply repeats itself, and the choice Americans face today is different in many respects than that faced in the past. To be sure, some of the general characteristics of the representative alternative can be learned from studying past representative systems, but key elements of these systems resulted from the distinct features of the parties at the time and therefore are not fully illustrative of the principle of representation itself. Virtually everyone who has studied party organizations over the past generation has taken note of the profound change in the motivations of members of party organizations. Parties today include a much larger share of individuals who have joined in order to promote policy objectives rather than to hold power and satisfy material wants. This shift in the character of party membership, based on a combination of changes in law, norms, and demography, makes it unlikely that patronage machines and bosses will ever again dominate American parties. If there is a danger in returning the selection process to party organizations today, it is less that of their excessive pragmatism than their ideological zeal.

Making a choice today between direct democracy and representation means, in some measure, legislating in the dark. Yet, barring the "worst case" of extreme parties—something seldom seen in American politics and something our electoral system seems to discourage—it is likely that a party-run representative nomination system can be counted on to produce certain general results. A representative system today would institute a degree of "peer review" by practicing politicians, diminish the pressures and incentives for presidential aspirants to attempt to create "new" coalitions, lessen the access of outsiders, and provide a modest supplement to the coordinating capacity of political parties in executive–legislative relations. In addition, there undoubtedly would be some unforeseen consequences accompanying any reinstitution of party prerogatives. This risk, in addition to one's assessment of the probable tendencies of a representative process, is one factor that legislators must weigh in deciding their preference.

FEASIBILITY

A number of commentators deny that the current nominating process offers any choice. A representative system, in their view, is an impossibility because our parties have become too weak to support the resumption of so critical a function as nominating presidential candidates. Nor, in this view, is there any hope for strengthening the parties, for the causes of their decline have little or nothing to do with structural features that are under the control of legislators, but derive instead from "uncontrollable" environmental factors such as the rise of modern communications technology and the advent in postindustrial society of an independent-minded "new class." These factors, it is claimed, obviate the need for parties by taking away functions they once performed and by creating political attitudes that are hostile to the idea of partisanship. As Arthur Schlesinger, Jr., has argued: "The attempt to shore up structure against loss of function is artificial and futile. The party system is simply no longer effective as an agency of mass mobilization, or an agency of candidate selection. . . ."[1]

This argument has had a great deal of appeal, in large part because it seems to explain so much while at the same time removing any responsibility on the part of legislators to take steps to strengthen parties. On closer analysis, however, the argument turns out to be much weaker than it appears, exaggerating the implications of party decline on the prospects for deliberate changes in the nominating process.

The main difficulty with this argument is that it assumes that a decline of party strength in some respects (as constraints on voting behavior or as agents for mobilizing the electorate) necessarily entails a weakening of parties in every other respect. There is, however, no logical reason for accepting such a conclusion. Parties have adapted to new circumstances in the past, giving up certain functions while retaining or gaining others. Indeed, as seen earlier (Chapter 6), parties were probably never quite so weak in the last decade as many made out, even though they had lost—or had been deprived of—many of their previous functions. The existence of a larger than usual percentage of independents in the electorate, however, is no reason to assume that parties cannot perform the nominating function. Parties today might have to take greater account of the preferences of independents or else face the threat of being contested by new parties or by "independent" candidacies, but this challenge hardly seems insurmountable. Ultimately, the determination of who should nominate is a legal and institutional matter defined by laws and rules that are subject to the legislator's control. Developments like television may require that parties adopt new rules in order to maintain their control, but it stretches the bounds of credulity to suggest that these technological innovations spell the parties' inevitable loss of the nominating function.

Moreover, the argument that socioeconomic forces must weaken parties as organizations capable of nominating contains a contradiction. As parties have lost the function of nominating, we have *not* experienced a total vacuum of organizational activity in the nominating process. On the contrary, in recent years there has been a growth in nonparty organizational efforts in the form of Political Action Committees, single-interest groups, and candidate-centered organizations. Indeed, the very same socioeconomic factor that many use to explain the decline of parties also is used to explain the growth of these other organizations: the activist and politically efficacious "new class" is said to shun partisan activity while moving quickly and easily to participate in other associations. Such an explanation, however, forces distinctions that are too fine for the broad sociological trends being discussed. Although the rise of the new class has introduced into the body politic a larger segment of the population concerned with promoting ideas and policies through organizational activities, it does not follow that this development must be at the expense of parties.

A simpler and more plausible explanation of the paradox of increased extrapartisan campaign activity while partisan activity has declined may be found in the current legal structure of the nominating system. People naturally seek to exert their energy and influence at the point where decisions are made; as parties have lost their control of the nominating process, organizational energies logically have shifted to accommodate the change in the locus of power. Accordingly, a return of the authority over nominations to the parties would mean that much of the organizational energy that currently is competing against parties would be channeled back into the parties. This understanding simply follows an old "law" of political science: If the loss of a function by an institution results in its devitalization, a restoration of function can lead to its revitalization.

Finally, it may be no accident that many of those who insist that it is impossible to institute representative decisionmaking also happen to believe that it is undesirable. Merely as a tactical ploy, the rhetorical direction of the determinist argument is to induce a state of passivity among those who might want to change the current system. Since action is futile, there is no reason to act. That so many of those who otherwise emphasize the power and efficacy of planned action to change institutions and social conditions support this argument should perhaps make one a bit suspicious; but in any case, advocates of a representative system owe it to themselves to put this determinist theory to the test. If they should succeed in accomplishing what is said to be impossible, it certainly would not be the first time that determinist hypotheses have fallen to the stubborn challenge of human will.

STRATEGY

Assuming that legislators decide to try to adopt a representative system, they still face the formidable problem of choosing the best plan and the best method for implementing it. Among proponents of representation, there seems to be widespread, although not universal, agreement that the change to a new system should be marginal, allowing for some further expression of rank-and-file sentiment through primaries, but reserving to representatives the prerogative of weighing the democratic preference against such other criteria as the qualifications of the candidates and the well-being of the party. This return to some variant of a "mixed" system, arranged carefully so as not to encourage the de facto selection of the nominee during the democratic phase, takes into account current popular notions of legitimacy and therefore offers the most promising practical approach under present circumstances.

The question of the best means for arriving at this goal has divided proponents of representation into two groups: those who favor using federal law to implement the change and those who prefer to rely on a combination of action on the part of national party organizations, state governments, and state party organizations. The issue here may rest finally on the practical consideration of which strategy is most likely to succeed. There are, however, three "rules" of prudence, which, all other things being equal, should be taken into consideration:

1. The strategy should have the least likelihood of producing unforeseen consequences.
2. The strategy should allow for reversing any change.
3. The strategy should be able to be implemented in the spirit of the end being sought.

These counsels of prudence clearly favor the second strategy of action by the parties and the states. This strategy has the advantage, if it works, of changing the character of the nominating process without changing the locus of decisionmaking authority to the federal government. Although change initiated by the federal government might be quicker and more certain to realize its objectives, it would alter fundamentally the status of parties and change, probably permanently, the decisionmaking authority for the nominating process. Furthermore, such a shift in authority is filled with possibilities for unforeseen consequences, including the spectacle of quadrennial struggles among political factions in Congress to change the law to favor particular candidates. Finally, it is impossible to overlook the contradiction that, if strength and independence of parties are the objectives, basing that strength on the "prop" of federal support would leave the parties hostage to a change in congressional sentiment. For their own sakes, the parties would do better to accomplish their objectives, if they can, through asserting their own authority as self-governing associations.

Because federal laws and regulations are already so much a part of the electoral process, it is clear that any major initiatives undertaken by the parties and states would require a modicum of federal cooperation. In particular, campaign finance legislation should be made consistent with the general spirit and objectives of any change. The specific alterations needed in the finance legislation can be determined only in conjunction with these changes, but the following proposals merit consideration:

- Move the date for receiving public funds to some time in April or May to accord with a new and shorter primary season.

- Increase significantly the contribution limitation for individuals and raise spending limits for the candidates, especially if there is evidence of significant independent PAC expenditures during primary contests.

- For the final campaign, allow national parties to contribute a significant amount to the campaigns of their nominees, again for the purpose of devaluing the impact of independent PAC expenditures.

The job of reforming the reforms cannot, however, stop at changing the rules and structures affecting the selection of delegates. If a representative decisionmaking process is to be reinstituted at the convention, attention must be paid to the character of the convention and its procedures. It is probably no accident that the size of the convention has expanded to unmanageable proportions at the very same time that it has lost its real authority. Lacking this authority, there was probably no good reason why the convention should not have been made as "representative" as possible. True representative bodies, however, must be formed to take into account not only how well they can reflect the sentiments of the public but also how well they can perform their appointed function. If some kind of deliberative decision on the nomination of presidential candidates is to be made at the convention, a smaller number of delegates will make the process somewhat less chaotic, even if much of the bargaining will, inevitably, take place off the floor of the convention hall. At the very least, the parties should resist any efforts to increase the number of delegates.

Even more important than the number of delegates, however, is the decorum of the convention, which in almost every conceivable way is influenced by the existence of journalists on the floor and in the aisles. Obviously, there is nothing "inevitable" in this kind of access. Despite what some might think, it would hardly be a violation of the First Amendment if the television cameras and journalists were asked to take their seats on the sidelines and not on the playing field. No less is demanded of the press at Super Bowl games.

* * *

The transformation of the presidential nominating process since 1968 was the centerpiece of a major attack on the entire principle of representation. This attack, made in the name of direct democracy, was undertaken with an underlying confidence in the efficacy of institutional change—indeed, often with the implicit belief that institutional change could be a substitute for politics. Reformers constantly attributed failures of policy during the past decade not to the misjudgment of fallible human beings but to institutional problems that could be remedied by simple democratic changes. For all the animus and passion that reformers sometimes directed against those in power, their belief, paradoxically, was in the perfectibility of man and the political system. Given the right institutions, the normal vices of political life and most of the great policy failures could be avoided.

After a brief experience with the results of the reforms, more and more leaders, including many former enthusiasts of reform, have begun to question their earlier premises and to rediscover the benefits of representative government. It is not that leaders today discount the importance of institutions; on the contrary, there is a growing understanding of their significance. But that understanding now includes an appreciation of the limits of institutions, an appreciation learned from the experience of a decade of constant institutional change. Today, it is understood that the methods of institutional decisionmaking cannot themselves solve all our problems; the most they can do is provide a better or worse setting in which citizens select their elected officials and in which these officials go about the task of attempting to govern wisely.

Legislators today face the formidable task of correcting the excesses of the past decade without being able to claim that these changes are panaceas for all the nation's problems and without being able to appeal through simplistic slogans to popular prejudices for greater democracy. Their challenge is the sober—and sobering—work of strengthening representative government.

NOTES

CHAPTER 1

1. Testimony of Austin Ranney before the Senate Committee on Rules and Administration, September 10, 1980 (mimeo).
2. The term "legislators" as it is used in this context refers to all those having the potential power to make changes in the rules and laws governing the nominating process. Among others, it includes members of Congress, of the state legislatures, party officials, convention delegates, members of special party commissions on selection, and state and federal judges.
3. Testimony of Robert Packwood before the Senate Committee on Rules and Administration, September 10, 1980 (mimeo).

CHAPTER 2

1. James Madison, *Notes of Debates in the Federal Constitution of 1787*, Adrienne Koch, ed. (New York: W. W. Norton, 1969), p. 595.
2. Cited in Neal Peirce, *The People's President* (New York: Simon & Schuster, 1968), p. 132.
3. After the Civil War, a number of states passed general statutes preventing fraud and intimidation in the conduct of party affairs. The general method of delegate selection, however, was left to the decision of the state parties. See Joseph R. Starr, "The Legal Status of American Political Parties," *American Political Science Review* 34 (June–August 1940): 439–55, 695–99.

4. *Ripon Society v. National Republican Party* (1975). The Court also re-
    fused to overturn the winner-take-all system of the Republican party in
    the case of *Graham v. March Fong Fu* (1975), *The New York Times*, Jan-
    uary 26, 1975. The Court's position is that most matters relating to dele-
    gate selection fall within the associational right of the party and "are
    matters for the political parties themselves to determine, and, if the parties
    permit it, for the states." *Graham v. March Fong Fu*, as quoted in *The
    New York Times* (January 26, 1975).
5. Republican rules adopted in 1884 codified the process that was in effect
    in most states. Delegates who were assigned at large to a state, that is, for
    the equivalent of senators in the electoral votes, would be chosen by the
    state convention. Delegates given for the representatives should be elected
    by the same manner that congressional candidates were nominated. See
    Richard C. Bain and Judith H. Parris, *Convention Decisions and Voting
    Records* (Washington, D. C.: Brookings Institution, 1973), p. 123.
6. James Bryce, *The American Commonwealth*, vol. 2 (London: Macmillan
    and Co., 1889), p. 180.
7. William R. Keech and Donald R. Matthews, *The Party's Choice* (Washing-
    ton, D. C.: Brookings Institution, 1976), p. 215.
8. James W. Davis, *Presidential Primaries: Road to the White House* (New
    York: Thomas Crowell, 1967), pp. 182-95.
9. Michael J. Robinson, "Television and American Politics: 1966-1976,"
    The Public Interest (Summer 1977): 20.

CHAPTER 3

1. For an excellent account of the intentions of those on the first reform
    commission, the McGovern-Fraser Commission, see Austin Ranney, *Cur-
    ing the Mischiefs of Faction* (Berkeley: University of California Press,
    1975), pp. 188-210.
2. Commission on Presidential Nomination and Party Structure, Morley Win-
    ograd, Chairman, *Openness, Participation and Party Building: Reforms for
    a Stronger Democratic Party* (Washington, D. C.: Democratic National
    Committee, 1978), p. 21.
3. The national Democratic party gave exemptions in 1980 to the states of
    Illinois and West Virginia.
4. According to the Democratic party rules in 1980, three-fourths of the del-
    egates had to be elected from units no larger than a congressional district,
    although single-member districts are not permitted. (Single-member dis-
    tricts would make proportional representation impossible.) The cut-off is
    determined on a sliding scale based on dividing the number of delegates
    running in a district by 100. The cut-off could not, however, go below

15 percent or above 25 percent. For the most complete compendium of delegate selection rules and laws in 1980, see Carol F. Casey, *Procedures for Selection of Delegates to the Democratic and Republican National Conventions* (Washington, D. C.: Congressional Research Service, October 22, 1979).

5. For an account of the history of proportional representation and an analysis of its effects in 1976, see Paul David and James Ceaser, *Proportional Representation in Presidential Nominating Politics* (Charlottesville: University Press of Virginia, 1980).

6. Before the 1970s, states could impose lengthy periods of party membership before allowing an individual to participate in a party's primary. The Supreme Court, in weighing the individual's right to vote against the state interest in protecting parties, came close in 1971 to eliminating most of these restrictions. (See *Bendinger v. Ogilvie*, 335 F. Supp. 572 (1971), at 576.) In 1973, however, the Court faced the issue directly and by a five-to-four decision upheld a New York law requiring an eight- to eleven-month registration period (*Rosario v. Rockefeller*, 93 S. Ct. 1245 [1973]).

7. Congressional Quarterly, *Weekly Report* (July 5, 1980):1874–75.

8. See David Paul, Ralph Goldman, and Richard Bain, *The Politics of National Party Conventions* (Washington, D. C.: Brookings Institution, 1960).

9. See the Commission on Party Structure and Delegate Selection (Senator George S. McGovern, chairman), *Mandate for Reform* (Washington, D. C.: Democratic National Committee, 1970).

10. *Id.* at 10.

11. Because it is the first of the delegate selection contests, the Iowa caucus is unlike any other in the nation in the extent of candidate attention and media coverage. Its characters are determined less by the fact that it is a caucus than by the fact that it comes first in the sequence.

12. *Cousins v. Wigoda*, 95 S. Ct. 541, 549.

13. Austin Ranney, *Participation in American Presidential Nomination, 1976* (Washington, D. C.: American Enterprise Institute, 1977), pp. 15–26.

14. Rules Committee Report, Democratic National Party (1980).

15. *Report on Commission on Democratic Selection of Presidential Nominees,* chairman, Harold Hughes. Reprinted in *Congressional Record* 114 (1968): 31547.

16. *Openness, Participation and Party Building,* supra note 2, at 18–20.

17. In primary states, 10 percent of each state's delegation must be composed of party and elected officials.

18. In 1968, 88 percent of the Republican governors, 55 percent of the Republican senators, and 31 percent of the Republican congressmen were in attendance at the convention. In 1980, the figures were, respectively, 74 percent, 63 percent, and 40 percent.

19. In this section, I have relied heavily on Thomas R. Marshall, "Nominating the President: A Model for the 1970's" (Paper presented at the annual meeting of the Southern Political Science Association, November 1–3, 1979).

20. It is important to remember, however, that voters, when they make up their minds in primaries—and for that matter in general elections as well—do not base their decision only on issues or ideology but also on their assessment of the qualifications of the individual candidate. Because this is the case, one cannot assume that all the people who voted for liberal candidates would transfer their support to a single liberal candidate if only one was running.

21. See F. Christopher Arterton, "The Media Politics of Presidential Campaign: A Study of the Carter Nomination Drive," in James David Barber, ed., *Race for the Presidency: The Media and the Nominating Process* (Englewood Cliffs, N. J.: Prentice–Hall, 1978), pp. 26–54.

22. See Michael Robinson, "Media Coverage in the Primary Campaign of 1976: Implications for Voters, Candidates, and Parties," in William Crotty, ed., *The Party Symbol* (San Francisco: W. H. Freeman, 1980), pp. 178–91.

23. *Ibid.*

24. See Nelson Polsby, "The News Media as an Alternative to Party in the Presidential Selection Process," in Robert Goldwin, ed., *Political Parties in the Eighties* (Washington, D. C.: American Enterprise Institute, 1980), pp. 50–66.

25. Thomas Patterson, *The Mass Media Elections* (New York: Praeger Publishers, 1980), p. 176.

26. This phenomenon is known as a "protest vote," and studies of the 1968 Democratic primary in New Hampshire indicate that many of the votes for Eugene McCarthy were protest votes against Lyndon Johnson. In 1980, some of the votes for Senator Edward Kennedy were protest votes against President Carter, but Kennedy was such a well-known and controversial figure in his own right that many voters chose to vote against him.

27. See Ranney, *Participation in American Presidential Nominations*, pp. 24–26; Congressional Quarterly, *Weekly Report* (July 5, 1980): 1875.

28. See Ranney, *Participation in American Presidential Nominations*. Richard Rubin argues that this decline is a result in part of the fact that some states only recently have adopted primaries and that in these states participation tends to be low. In states that have had primaries consistently since 1948, participation has increased. Rubin attributes this difference to the need of voters to become used to presidential primaries. See Richard Rubin, "Presidential Primaries: Communities, Dimensions of Change, and Political Implications," in Crotty, ed., *The Party Symbol*, pp. 126–47.

29. See Rubin, "Presidential Primaries."

30. For evidence that, at least in 1972, the primary voters basically were representative of the party voters in the general election, see Herbert M. Kritzer,

"The Representativeness of the 1977 Presidential Primaries," in Crotty, ed., *The Party Symbol*, pp. 148–53. This article represents only the beginning of an effort to answer this question.

31. The earlier laws are discussed in Herbert E. Alexander, *Money in Politics* (Washington, D. C.: Public Affairs Press, 1977), pp. 183–229.

32. Robert La Follette, *Autobiography* (Madison, Wisc.: Robert M. La Follette Co., 1913), p. 636.

33. See William Crotty, *Political Reform and the American Experiment* (New York: Thomas Y. Crowell, 1977), p. 106.

34. Herbert E. Alexander, "Financing the Campaigns and Parties of 1980" (Paper presented at Sangamon State University, Springfield, Illinois, December 3, 1980).

35. *Ibid.*

CHAPTER 4

1. Tom Wicker, "The Elections: Why the System Has Failed," *New York Review of Books* (August 14, 1980): 20.

2. Sometimes the institutional aspects of the system may themselves be continually subject to change. Where this occurs, and where rules shift as readily as strategies, the "institution" is in a state of chaos and performs no structuring effect.

3. Austin Ranney, *The Federalization of Presidential Primaries* (Washington, D. C.: American Enterprise Institute, 1978), pp. 20–21.

4. First message to Congress, December 8, 1829.

5. Martin Van Buren, *Inquiry into the Origin and Course of Political Parties in the United States* (New York: Hurd and Houghton, 1867), pp. 3–4.

6. For a discussion of Americans' views on parties, see Austin Ranney, *Curing the Mischiefs of Faction* (Berkeley: University of California Press, 1975), pp. 22–57.

7. Thomas Ritchie, "Congressional Caucus No. 3," *Richmond Enquirer* (January 2, 1824); Ranney, *The Federalization of Presidential Primaries*, p. 34.

8. Kirk Potter and Donald Johnson, *National Party Platforms* (Urbana: University of Illinois Press, 1956), p. 175.

9. Robert La Follette, *Autobiography* (Madison, Wisc.: Robert M. La Follette Co., 1913), pp. 197–98.

10. *Report of the Commission on the Democratic Selection of Presidential Nominees* (Hughes Commission), reprinted in *Congressional Record* 114 : 315–46.

11. Kenneth A. Bode and Carol F. Casey, "Party Reform: Revisionism Revised," in Robert Goldwin, ed., *Political Parties in the Eighties* (Washington, D.C.: American Enterprise Institute, 1980), p. 19.

12. The poll data are collected in Joseph B. Gorman, *Federal Presidential Primary Proposals, 1911–1979* (Congressional Research Service, Library of Congress, JK 2017 A 80–53GOV, Washington. D.C., November 1980).

13. The more polling data one looks at, however, the more confusing the picture becomes. In 1977, when NBC asked people whether they would prefer a national primary to the current state-by-state primary system, the results of the survey were almost an exact tie. And this year, before the primaries got under way, a *Los Angeles Times* poll showed the American people to be very satisfied with the current system, a finding that seems to contradict the Gallup result. Clearly, in this area the results of the polls reflect the way the questions are posed, and great care must be taken to analyze the particular opinion that is measured in each case. See *Los Angeles Times* (January 27, 1980).

14. E. E. Schattschneider, *Party Government* (New York: Farrar and Rinehart, 1940), p. 60.

15. See Austin Ranney, "Candidate Selection," in David Butler, Howard Penniman, and Austin Ranney, eds., *Democracy at the Polls* (Washington, D. C.: American Enterprise Institute, 1981), pp. 75–106.

16. V. O. Key, *Politics. Parties and Pressure Groups*, 5th ed. (New York: Thomas Y. Crowell, 1964), pp. 254–281.

17. Caucus participation rates, as noted in Chapter 3, are much lower on an average than participation rates in primaries. In 1976, the average turnout in Democratic nonprimary states, based on a percentage of the voting age population, was 1.9 percent versus 18.6 percent in the closed primary states. Comparable figures are not available for the Republican party. For a discussion of the turnout data, see Austin Ranney, *Participation in American Presidential Nominations, 1976* (Washington, D. C.: American Enterprise Institute, 1977), pp. 24–26.

18. Adam Smith, *The Wealth of Nations* (New York: Modern Library, 1937), p. 67.

19. William R. Keech and Donald R. Matthews, *The Party's Choice* (Washington, D. C.: Brookings Institution, 1976), p. 270.

20. Theodore J. Lowi, "Party, Policy and Constitution in America," in William N. Chambers and Walter Dean Burnham, eds., *The American Party Systems*, 2nd ed. (New York: Oxford University Press, 1975), pp. 246–48.

21. *The New York Times* (January 27, 1980): sec. 1, p. 16.

22. Stephen Hess, *The Presidential Campaign* (Washington, D. C.: Brookings Institution, 1974), p. 42.

23. Malcolm Jewell, "Presidential Selection," *Society* (July/August 1980): 48.

24. Geoffrey Smith, "The Lessons To Be Learnt from the American Way of Choosing a Leader," *The Times* (September 5, 1980).

25. Austin Ranney, Testimony before the Senate Committee on Rules and Administration, September 10, 1980.

26. Norman Ornstein, Robert Peabody, and David Rhode, "The Changing Senate: From the 1950s to the 1970s," Lawrence C. Dodd and Bruce I. Oppenheimer, eds., in *Congress Reconsidered*, (New York: Praeger Publishers, 1977), p. 17.

27. *The Virginia Enquirer* (December 23, 1823).

28. Everett C. Ladd, "A Better Way to Pick Our Presidents," *Fortune* (May 5, 1980): 133-34.

29. Bode and Casey, "Party Reform," p. 4.

30. James Sundquist, *Dynamics of the Party System* (Washington, D. C.: Brookings Institution, 1973), p. 307.

31. Woodrow Wilson, *Constitutional Government in the United States* (New York: Columbia University Press, 1961), pp. 204-05.

32. Richard Rose, "Governments against Sub-Governments," in Richard Rose and Ezra Suleiman, eds., *Presidents and Prime Ministers* (Washington, D.C.: American Enterprise Institute, 1980), pp. 313-316.

33. Jeffrey Fischel, "From Campaign Promise to Presidential Performance" (Paper for a Colloquium of the Woodrow Wilson Center, Washington, D. C., June 20, 1978).

34. Richard Neustadt, *Presidential Power* (New York: John Wiley & Sons, 1976), pp. 19-22.

35. Alexis de Tocqueville, *Democracy in America*, J. P. Mayer, ed. (New York: Doubleday, 1969), p. 135.

CHAPTER 5

1. Statement of Lowell Weicker, Jr., before the Senate Committee on Rules and Administration, September 10, 1980 (mimeo).

2. Edward Banfield, "In Defense of the American Party System," in Robert Goldwin, ed., *Political Parties in the Eighties* (Washington, D. C.: American Enterprise Institute, 1980), p. 133.

3. See Joseph B. Gorman, *Federal Presidential Primary Proposals, 1911-1979* (Congressional Research Service, Library of Congress, JK 2071 A 80-53 GOV, Washington, D.C., November, 1980).

4. Austin Ranney, *The Federalization of Presidential Primaries* (Washington, D. C.: American Enterprise Institute, 1978), p. 1. It should be noted that the number of presidential primary bills introduced in the last two Congresses declined somewhat from the rate over the first part of the decade.

5. See Article II, Sections 1 and 2.

6. See James Ceaser, *Presidential Selection, Theory and Development* (Princeton, N. J.: Princeton University Press, 1979), pp. 123-69.

7. *United States v. Classic*, 311 U. S. 299 (1941), at 314-17. See also Ranney's discussion of this issue in *Federalization of Presidential Primaries*, pp. 9-12.

8. *Oregon v. Mitchell*, 400 U. S. 112 (1970), at 124.

9. *Burroughs v. United States*, 290 U. S. 534 (1934), at 545.

10. For evidence and opinions suggesting that Congress does have the power to legislate in this area, see *Buckley v. Valeo*, 424 U. S. 1 (1976), at 13–14; James F. Blumstein, "Party Reform, the Winner-Take-All-Primary and the California Delegate Challenge: The Gold Rush Revisited," *Vanderbilt Law Review* 25 (1972):1975; Ranney, *Federalization of Presidential Primaries*, p. 12.

11. See William J. Crotty, *Political Reform and the American Experiment* (New York: Thomas Y. Crowell, 1977), pp. 255–61; Charles Longley, "Party Reform and the Republican Party" (Paper presented at the annual meeting of the American Political Science Association, September 1978).

12. I have chosen here elements from Senator Packwood's optional regional primary plan (S. 964 in 1980) and transformed them into a mandatory proposal. There are mandatory proposals that resemble the Packwood plan, for example, a plan introduced by Richard Ottinger in 1977 (H. R. 4519), but they contain minor elements that are controversial and that would detract from the general direction of this study.

13. Raymond E. Wolfinger and Steven Rosenstone, *Who Votes?* (New Haven: Yale University Press, 1980).

14. Ranney, *Federalization of Presidential Primaries*, p. 37.

15. William Keech and Donald Matthews, *The Party's Choice* (Washington, D. C.: Brookings Institution, 1976), p. 245.

16. Cited in Stephen Hess, *The Presidential Campaign*, rev. ed. (Washington, D. C.: Brookings Institution, 1978), pp. 73–74.

17. Ranney, *Federalization of Presidential Primaries*, p. 3, detects such a change in one of the leading textbooks on American elections (Nelson Polsby and Aaron Wildavsky, *Presidential Elections*, 4th ed. (New York: Scribner and Sons, 1976). In the fourth edition, published in 1976, these authors write:

    > . . . if the existing and evolving presidential nominating process also weakens parties, and if it, in addition, enthrones purists over politicians, then given this unfortunate choice, a more direct relationship between candidates and their countrymen might be lesser evil.

18. H. R. 4329 (1977).

19. Senator Packwood has introduced plans along these lines for many years, the latest in 1979–80, S. 964.

20. Jeane J. Kirkpatrick and Michael J. Malbin, *The Presidential Nominating Process, Can it be Improved?* (Washington, D. C.: American Enterprise Institute, 1980), pp. 16–17.

21. *Id.* at 18–19.

22. Everett C. Ladd, "A Better Way to Pick Our Presidents," *Fortune* (May 5, 1980): 132–42.

23. Terry Sanford, "Picking the Presidents," *Atlantic Monthly* (August 1980): 29–33.

24. *Ibid.*

25. *Ibid.*

26. Tom Wicker, "The Elections: Why the System Has Failed," *New York Review of Books* (August 14, 1980): 15.

27. *President's Commission for a National Agenda for the Eighties, the Electoral and Democratic Process in the Eighties* (Washington, D. C.: U. S. Government Printing Office, 1980), pp. 15–16.

28. Donald M. Fraser, "Democratizing the Democratic Party," in Goldwin, ed., *Political Parties in the Eighties*, p. 130.

29. This suggestion has been made by Joel Fleishman, director of Duke University's Institute of Policy Sciences and Public Affairs.

CHAPTER 6

1. William J. Crotty and Gary C. Jacobson, *American Parties in Decline* (Boston: Little, Brown & Co., 1980).

2. The Gallup Poll, June 13–16, cited in *Public Opinion Magazine* (December/January 1981): 19. After June, Anderson began to slip steadily in the polls. He ended up receiving 6.6 percent of the vote against Reagan's 50.8 percent and Carter's 41.0 percent.

3. Austin Ranney, *Curing the Mischiefs of Faction* (Berkeley: University of California Press, 1975), p. 22.

4. Jeane J. Kirkpatrick, *Dismantling the Parties* (Washington, D.C.: American Enterprise Institute, 1978), pp. 2, 3, 20.

5. Everett C. Ladd, *Transformations of the American Party System*, 2d ed. (New York: W. W. Norton, 1978), pp. 329, 331.

6. Arthur Schlesinger, Jr., "The Crisis of the Party System II," *The Wall Street Journal* (May 10, 1978).

7. Alexis de Tocqueville, *Democracy in America*, George Lawrence, trans. (New York: Doubleday, 1964), pp. 174–75.

8. James Sundquist, *Dynamics of the Party System* (Washington, D. C.: Brookings Institution, 1973), pp. 281, 296.

9. This immediate legal authority is limited by Supreme Court decision on the Constitution, but for the most part, the Supreme Court in recent years has protected the quasi-private status of the national parties as self-governing associations. See especially *Cousins v. Wigoda*, 419 U. S. 477 (1975), at 490.

10. Such a law in the United States would almost certainly be declared unconstitutional as a violation of the First Amendment. However, there has been much talk about finding some method in America of preventing the

reporting of election results in states in the East from potentially affecting voting behavior in states in the West, where the polls close later.

11. The visible and measurable indices of party decline, such as partisan identification and party-line voting in Congress, have been catalogued by numerous scholars in the past decade. See, for example, Austin Ranney, "The Political Parties: Reform and Decline," in Anthony King, ed., *The New American Political System* (Washington, D. C.: American Enterprise Institute, 1978), pp. 213–48.

12. See James Q. Wilson, "American Politics Then and Now," *Commentary* (February 1979): 41.

13. James Sundquist, "Congress and the President: Enemies or Partners?" in Lawrence Dodd and Bruce Oppenheimer, eds., *Congress Reconsidered* (New York: Praeger Publishers, 1977), pp. 241, 242.

14. *Gallup Poll Index*, Report no. 181, September 1980, p. 19. For the best general description of voting behavior and trends in the 1980 election, see William Schneider, "The November 4 Vote: What Did It Mean?" in Austin Ranney, ed., *America at the Polls* (Washington, D. C.: American Enterprise Institute, 1981).

15. Walter Dean Burnham, "American Politics in the 1970s: Beyond Party," in David Abbot and Edward Rogowsky, eds., *Political Parties* (Chicago: Rand–McNally, 1978), p. 370.

16. *The Washington Post* (December 10, 1980); *The Washington Post* (July 3, 1981).

17. Samuel Beer, "In Search of a New Public Philosophy," in King, ed., *The New American Political System*, pp. 5–44.

18. Harvey C. Mansfield, Jr., "The American Election: Towards Constitutional Democracy," *Government and Opposition* 16, no. 1 (Winter 1981): 18.

CHAPTER 7

1. Arthur Schlesinger, Jr., "The Crisis of the Party System II," *The Wall Street Journal* (May 14, 1979).

INDEX

ABOUT THE AUTHOR

James W. Ceaser is associate professor of government, Woodrow Wilson Department of Government and Foreign Affairs, University of Virginia. He is the author of the recently published and highly praised *Presidential Selection: Theory and Development* (Princeton, 1979), which examines the American nominating process in a theoretical and historical context. Mr. Ceaser's papers and articles on this subject have influenced the work of a number of committees and commissions investigating this subject.